Better Homes and Gardens®

The Joy of Patchwork

MURDOCH BOOKS®

Sydney • London • Vancouver

Contents

ℚUILTS   21

𝒲ALLHANGINGS   45

𝒞USHIONS   57

A Little Patchwork History

I've had a heap o' comfort all my life makin' quilts, and now in my old age I wouldn't take a fortune for 'em … You see, some folks has albums to put folks' pictures in to remember 'em by and some folks has a book and writes down the things that happen every day so they won't forgit 'em; but honey, these quilts is my albums and my di'ries, and whenever the weather's bad and I can't git out to see folks, I jest spread out my quilts and look at 'em and study over 'em and it's just like goin' back fifty or sixty years and livin' my life over again.

'AUNT JANE OF KENTUCKY', WRITTEN IN 1898 BY ELIZA CALVERT HALL

One of the most well-known pieces of writing about quilts, this extract typifies the feeling many people had about their patchwork and quilting. Because the quilts were made from worn-out clothes or bedspreads or curtains, they held many memories and were greatly valued and passed down from mother to daughter.

In Australia, patchwork was mostly used for bush rugs or waggas, often with a sacking backing. They weren't made for show, they were utilitarian: used as a spare blanket or for camping trips. Other, more decorative quilts were made from shiny fabrics and were heavily embroidered, often bearing mottos or stories.

Patchwork developed from necessity. The American pilgrims brought clothing, quilts and blankets with them to their new land but because England at first outlawed the manufacture of cloth in the colonies, they had to make their new clothes out of patches of worn-out clothes or bedclothes.

Even when they did start to grow their own cotton and spin wool from their own sheep, there was not enough cloth to make European-style quilts until the Industrial Revolution. The earliest American quilts were made from scraps of fabric, trimmed and stitched into crazy patches. Slowly the women began to arrange the pieces into geometric patterns and designs. This is how many of the most well-known patchwork designs came into being.

It was the custom in America until about 1900 for a young girl to make twelve quilts before she was old enough to marry. With each new quilt the pattern was more intricate so that she learnt the skills of the craft gradually while making quilts to take to her new home. When she became engaged, the thirteenth quilt, the Marriage Quilt, which was always an elaborate masterpiece, was made. This was the only quilt that could include hearts and other symbols of love. It was often made by friends and relations and presented to the bride as a wedding present.

Quilting bees, when women would come from far away to get together and stitch, being 'as busy as bees', were an opportunity to socialise, make new friends and swap fabric pieces, patterns and ideas. They were a popular way of coping with isolation and loneliness and were especially common among Amish women.

While many fabrics have been used in patchwork, the most popular, and as history has shown us, long lasting choice, was 100 per cent cotton. It is still the most favoured fabric among patchworkers. By the 1850s fabric had become an affordable commodity and most women could purchase fabric specifically for quilt making. With this change of fortune quiltmakers were able to repeat a pattern in a particular colour and fabric and thus create a geometric design. Today we can often identify the age of a quilt by the fabrics used. The Depression quilts of the 1930s are easy to spot because of the predominance of bright cheery colours and three very favoured patterns of the time: Grandmother's Fan, Dresden Plate and Grandmother's Flower Garden.

I have found nothing so desirable for summer covers as the old-fashioned scrap quilt of which our mothers were so proud. Every girl should piece one at least to carry away to her husband's home. And if her lot happens to be cast among strangers, the quilt when she unfolds it will seem like the face of a familiar friend, bringing up a host of memories too sacred to intrude upon.

ANNIE CURD, *GOOD HOUSEKEEPING*, 1888

POSTAGE STAMP QUILT, *see page 28*

Today we're still fascinated by patchwork and quilting. While many other crafts have come and gone, patchwork and quilting have not only survived, there's a revival of interest in them—books are being published, exhibitions are being held, classes are being given all around the country. And those humble quilts made by pioneer women, often from men's suiting fabrics, are now proudly hanging in our art galleries and museums.

The patterns presented here are meant to supply inspiration as well as instructions. Once you've learned the basics you can make up your own patterns, choose fabric and colour combinations that are pleasing to you and embellish and decorate your work in your own particular style.

Patchwork isn't confined to quilts. You can make patchwork cushion covers, wall-hangings, clothing, even Christmas decorations. Patchwork is a time-consuming activity, especially when it's done by hand, but if you use good-quality fabrics, your work will last for generations. Always sign and date your patchwork; it is, after all, a work of art.

Australia's Quiltmakers

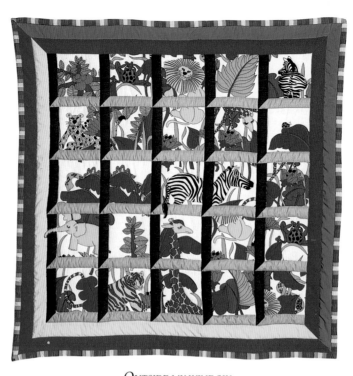

OUTSIDE MY WINDOW
107 x 107 cm, 1989
Made by Pam Halcro. A traditional Attic Window design, from Diana Leone's book, 'Attic Window'.

Quilts are a relatively new art form in Australia. Interest in them began in the late seventies when a few classes started up around the country, and in the eighties exponents of the art, especially from America, began to arrive here to give demonstrations and lectures. Now the National Gallery exhibits examples of Australian quilts, wallhangings and embroidery. And, as the examples in this book show, Australia's quiltmakers and patchworkers are extremely talented. Quilting and patchwork is, like any work of art, a way to express yourself.

It's painstaking work, but quiltmakers will tell you it's compulsive (many of them work long into the night), therapeutic and soothing. Once you've made your first patchwork piece you'll find it difficult to stop. Many quiltmakers complain of not having enough room to store their fabrics and of not being able to leave a fabric shop without at least one length of material tucked under their arm (which some of them hide guiltily from their families).

Like all textile arts, the choice of fabric is most important, not just the colour and texture, but the value (lightness and darkness of a colour). Manipulation of values can create a feeling of perspective in your work—dark value fabrics appear to recede into the background, those with a light value to jump out. Modern quiltmakers often use all sorts of other art forms such as painting and screen printing as well as appliqué and embroidery in their work.

The quilts and wallhangings featured in this book show the work of a few of Australia's best quiltmakers. Some of them have been making quilts for years and have exhibited widely, some are novices to the art. Some use traditional patterns, some design their own. Some hand-stitch every piece, some machine-stitch and some use a mixture of both. There are no rules.

Every year the Australian Quilters' Guild holds an exhibition of quilts and wallhangings. For information write to The Quilters' Guild Inc, P.O. Box 654, Neutral Bay Junction, NSW, 2089.

FROM FOREST FLOOR TO CANOPY—RAINFOREST III
156 x 226 cm, 1991
Made by Irma Chelsworth. This original design is the third in Irma's rainforest series.

ALL THE FLOWERS BLOOM IN SPRING
167 x 284 cm, 1990
Made by Keasi Uluitoga. This is Keasi's first quilt; it contains over 8000 pieces, many of them hand-dyed scraps.

INNER SPACE, OUTER SPACE
143 x 205 cm, 1990/91
Made by Christa Roksandic. An original design, machine-pieced and hand-quilted.

To Baltimore with love
208 x 244 cm, 1990–91
Made by Val Moore. The traditional Baltimore-style quilt, from an American pattern by Patricia Cox.

BALTIMORE
271 x 271 cm, 1990
Made by Kim McLean. 'Baltimore' quilts are appliquéd, and are so-called because they were first made in
Baltimore, Maryland in the 1830s.

A TISKET, A TASKET, FILL UP CASEY'S BASKETS
212 x 244 cm, 1990
Made by Kim McLean. The name comes from a nursery rhyme Kim McLean's daughter sang, while Kim arranged the eighty-five blocks on the floor.

NUDGING AND FUDGING
203 x 244 cm, 1990/91
Made by Avis Batcheldor. A sampler quilt using blocks mainly from Jinny Beyer's book.

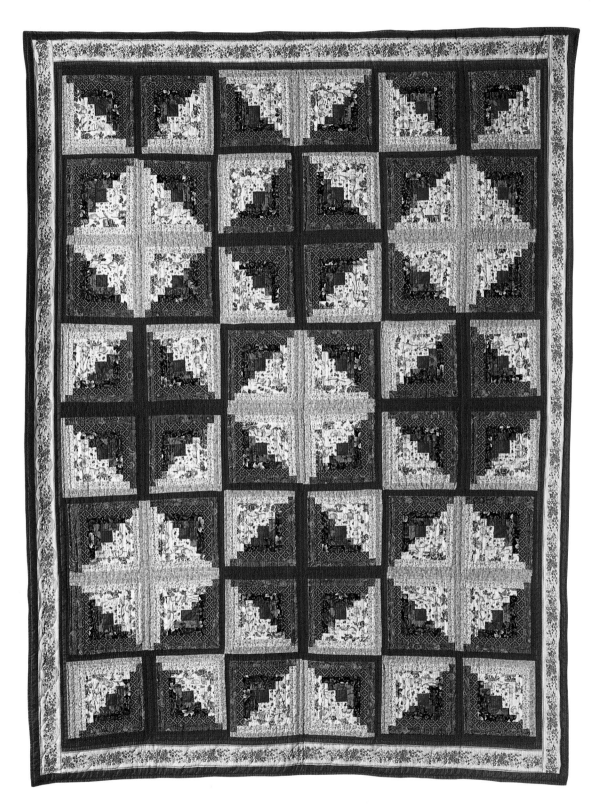

LOG CABIN
152 x 194 cm, 1990/91
Made by Margaret Zucker. The quilting gives an interesting effect on the plain fabric used on the back of the quilt.

TABLE TOP STILL LIFE
108 x 113 cm
Made by Deborah Brearley. This piece was screen printed, painted, machine-stitched, appliquéd and quilted.

CHECKING WITH IVY
144 x 144 cm, 1990
Made by Phyllis Sullivan. The use of plaids in this quilt produces a very interesting effect.

DOUBLE BLUE STAR
238 x 240 cm, 1990
Made by Elizabeth Rose. Striped fabric has been cleverly used here by 'splitting' the diamond block.

Quilts

Without question the ultimate patchwork and quilting project is the quilt. You can choose your patchwork design from hundreds of traditional and modern patterns, or if you're really adventurous, make your own. Quilts can be made with new, co-ordinating fabrics, or old dress remnants, but make sure they're of similar weight. A quilt is a work of art, so always sign and date it for future generations.

STRAIGHT FURROW QUILT

This dramatic arrangement of the Log Cabin design is called Straight Furrow. The careful placement of the shaded blocks gives diagonal strips of light and dark fabric which is even more obvious when you stand a few feet away from the quilt. The blocks are hand quilted in the middle of each strip.

Materials
Light and dark fabric scraps; calico; cotton backing fabric; polyester wadding; bias binding.

Instructions
Cut and piece log cabin blocks to the desired size (see page 25 for Log Cabin construction). Assemble the quilt top in a pattern to create diagonal light and dark lines running upwards from the lower left to the upper right (see colour picture).

Sandwich wadding between the quilt top and the backing fabric. Baste and quilt as desired following instructions on page 101. Finish the edges with bias binding.

Log Cabin Designs

The Log Cabin block is one of the most popular patchwork patterns. It lends itself to many variations, some of which are shown below. It is a symbol of the American frontier, the strips of fabric representing the interlocking logs of a cabin. It is made by sewing strips (the logs) around a centre square (the cabin's heart). Usually the block is made from half light-coloured and half dark-coloured fabric.

THE LOG CABIN PATCH

The Log Cabin Patch
This is the basic Log Cabin design. Dark fabric strips are placed on one half of the block, light fabric on the other, separating the block into two triangles of colour.

Light and Dark
This is also known as *Sunshine and Shadow*. The light side of each block is made by alternating light- and medium-coloured fabric strips; the dark side is made by alternating dark and medium coloured strips.

Straight Furrow
The light and dark diagonal strips of fabric represent the patterns made in a plowed field. Each block is the same, made of half light, half dark fabric. The design is achieved by turning the blocks to form strips of light and dark.

LIGHT AND DARK

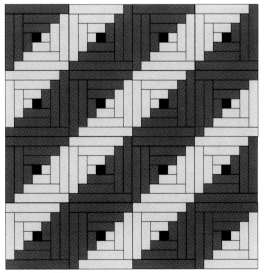

STRAIGHT FURROW

Streak of Lightning
Another simple Log Cabin design, this is made in a similar way to *Straight Furrow*, in that the blocks are the same. The pattern is achieved by turning the blocks to give the jagged, zig-zag look of lightning.

Barn Raising
A pattern of light and dark concentric diamonds depict the beams of a new barn. Half of each block is made from dark-coloured fabric, half from light-coloured and the blocks are turned to achieve the pattern.

Courthouse Steps
This is a variation of the Log Cabin design. Strips of the same fabric, in the same order, are placed on opposite rather than adjacent sides of the centre square.

Pineapple
This is also called *Windmill Blades* and *Maltese Cross*. It is an intricate variation of Log Cabin, best attempted only by experienced patchworkers.

HOW TO PIECE LIGHT AND DARK LOG CABIN BLOCKS

1. Cut a calico backing square the size of the finished block, adding 6 mm seam allowance. Mark the centre by drawing diagonal lines from opposite corners: where the lines intersect is the exact centre. Cut a small square of dark fabric, adding 6 mm seam allowance. Fold the square in half and press. Fold the square diagonally and mark its centre. Baste the square onto the calico, exactly matching centres.

With right sides together, pin and machine or handstitch a dark strip to one side of the centre square, using 6 mm seams. Trim the strip so that it is exactly as long as the square. Select a second dark strip. With right sides together, pin strip at right angles to the first strip. Cut a third strip, this time in light fabric, positioning it at right angles to the preceding strip. Repeat for the fourth log. We have pieced the strips counter-clockwise. They can also be worked clockwise but either way you must be consistent.

2. Continue adding logs to the square until you reach the desired size.

3. Because we started with a short dark strip and finished with a longer light strip, the dark half is smaller than the light half. This can be varied by beginning with light strips rather than dark, or by starting with a dark strip then two light strips and a second dark strip. This sequence is repeated until the piece is finished. The proportion of the light and dark halves will change.

1

2

3

ℬLAZING ℐTAR ℬEAUTY

ℕot many of us would think of using a powder blue printed fabric as a background to rich reds, deep browns and warm ochres, yet here it works exceptionally well, the soft blue background being a perfect foil for the striking pattern. The nine motifs are individually pieced before being joined to make the quilt top.

FINISHED SIZE: approx. 240 cm square.
NOTE: Use 6 mm seams throughout.

Materials

115 cm-wide cotton fabric in following amounts and colours: 3.2 m dark brown print; 3.2 m mid-blue print; 3 m white with brown polka dots; 2.8 m rust print; 2 m brown floral; 90 cm navy print; 45 cm beige print; 45 cm red print; 5.5 m backing fabric; polyester wadding to measure 240 cm square; thread.

Instructions

First enlarge block pattern from diagram by drawing a new grid on a large sheet of paper to scale given. Carefully copy design onto enlarged grid. Then cut out one template each for pieces A to H. For each quilt block (there are nine blocks in all), allowing 6 mm for seam beyond edge of template, cut A and B from red print fabric, C and G from brown dot fabric, F from dark brown print and H from mid-blue print. Cut eight D pieces from beige print and eight from brown floral. Cut eight E pieces from navy print and eight from rust print.

To piece the blocks, work in rounds from the centre A, stitching H pieces in last. For D and E rounds, alternate colours of pieces. Also alternate placement of darker-coloured pieces on each round so beige print falls below navy print and brown floral falls below rust print. Stitch quilt blocks together into three rows of three.

For borders, cut two 9 cm-wide strips each of the following lengths from specified fabrics: brown floral, 181 and 196 cm; blue print, 196 and 211 cm; rust print, 211 and 226 cm; brown print, 226 and 241 cm. Starting with brown floral, stitch shorter strips to side edges of quilt top, then longer strips to top and bottom edges. Then stitch remaining strips in

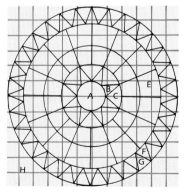

1 square = 5 cm

place in order of listing. When quilt top is complete, assemble layers. Place back, wrong side up, on flat surface and smooth over. Cover with wadding (pieced or trimmed to the size of the top), then add quilt top, right side up. Pin layers together. Establish centre points on all sides and baste from top to bottom and side to side, then from corner to corner diagonally.

Choose a quilting pattern that suits the pieced top; use pictures for reference. Quilt through all layers using fine, running stitches (three or four to 1 cm). Use a short, sharp needle and a good-quality, strong thread in either cotton or polyester. Machine quilt if desired with a heavy needle and large stitch (see page 102).

To make a fabric binding for a quilt, cut strips 5 cm wide and join them into a strip long enough to go completely around quilt. Cut either with the grain or on the bias. Pin binding to quilt top, right sides together, starting in the middle of one side; mitre corners as you go. Machine-stitch the binding in place. Trim quilt edge. Fold binding to back, pin it in place and hem by hand to the backing.

POSTAGE STAMP QUILT

Aptly named because it is made of 2 cm squares, the postage stamp quilt pattern is not for the faint-hearted. The central diamonds are pieced using printed fabrics and the outer diamonds are defined by four rows of vibrant, solid colours. Bands of blue and white then link all the diamonds together. For a less time-consuming version simply increase the size of the squares.

FINISHED SIZE: approx. 230 cm square.

NOTE: Diagram is the pattern for one block, measuring 46 cm square. There are 25 blocks in all in quilt. The strip outlined in heavy lines on right side of block pattern should be included only for blocks which fall on right side of quilt. Similarly, the strip outlined in heavy lines at bottom of block pattern should be included only for blocks which fall at the bottom of the quilt. For all other blocks, leave off.

Materials

115 cm-wide plain cotton fabrics in following quantities and colours: black, 20 cm; blue, 1 m; white, 1.6 m; red, 1.5 m; pink, 1.3 m; lavender, 1.2 m; orange, 1 m. If printed parts of diamonds are to be identical you'll need the following quantities of 115 cm-wide fabric each in a different design: 80 cm; 70 cm; 50 cm; 40 cm; 20 cm. You'll also need 5 m of 115 cm-wide backing fabric; 230 cm square of polyester wadding if desired; thread.

Instructions

Cut fabrics into 3.2 cm squares (this includes 6 mm seam allowance). Carefully following diagram, set out the fabric squares for each block as they will appear in the quilt. Use 6 mm seam allowances throughout and begin at the bottom left-hand corner of the block. Stitch together a horizontal row of squares. Work your way up in sequence completing all rows then seam them together to make a block. Make 25 blocks in all and finally join them together in five rows of five.

Finish according to *Blazing Star Beauty* instructions (see page 26). Catch quilt top to backing by hand with a few stitches through the black squares.

Teddy Bear Cot Quilt

*D*esigned specifically to be cot size, this bears and bows quilt will quickly become the favourite with small children. Make it cheery and fun by using bright, bold colours for the bears and sashings.

FINISHED SIZE: approx. 115 x 100 cm.

Materials

Cotton fabrics (115 cm wide) in following amounts and colours: 1 m green polka dot; 2 m medium green; 1.2 m white; 30 cm each of yellow polka dot, red print, green polka dot, orange polka dot, yellow, orange and red; 2 m backing fabric; 1.4 m binding fabric; No. 8 black pearl embroidery thread; 115 x 100 cm polyester wadding; ribbon.

Instructions

Cut nine white blocks, each 29 x 24 cm. For sashing strips, cut long strips of green fabric 5.7 cm wide and long strips of green polka dot fabric 4.2 cm wide. Using 6 mm seams, sew a polka dot strip between two green strips; final width of pieced strip is 13.2 cm. You'll need 6.8 m of sashing strip in all. Cut strips to approximate length when assembling quilt top. Also cut four 12 cm squares of green polka dot fabric, adding 6 mm seam allowance to all sides.

Enlarge diagram for bear appliqué. Cut two ears, arms and feet, and one nose and body shape for each bear from orange, yellow, red and green fabrics. Use polka dot and print fabric for bodies; cut remaining shapes from solid colours. Add 6 mm seam allowances to each piece.

To appliqué bear, turn under seam allowances on all pieces; baste. Pin body of bear to white background block (longer side of block should be placed vertically). Tuck ears beneath head as shown; whip-stitch body and ears in place. Appliqué nose to face; sew paws in place, varying positions as shown in photograph.

Using pearl cotton, satin-stitch eyes and nose; chain-stitch mouth.

Appliqué nine blocks.

To assemble quilt top, lay out three rows of three bear blocks each. Cut pieced sashing strips into six 29 cm lengths (measure blocks to be sure dimensions are correct). Stitch two pieced strips between three blocks for each row.

To join rows, make two horizontal sashing strips. Sew these long horizontal strips between the three rows of blocks, then topstitch small green polka dot squares at each sashing strip intersection, turning seam allowance to wrong side.

Finally, cut and stitch pieced sashing strips to top and bottom of quilt, then to sides. Piece backing fabric to match size of quilt top. Sandwich wadding

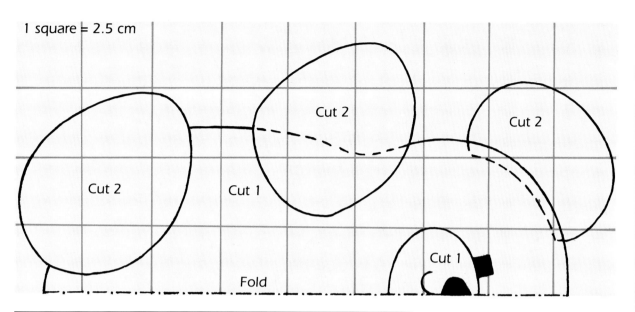

1 square = 2.5 cm

Cut 2

Cut 2

Cut 2

Cut 2

Cut 1

Cut 1

Fold

between quilt top and backing. Baste all layers together and quilt.

On white blocks, outline-quilt 3 mm beyond outline of bear using green thread. Then quilt blocks in diagonal rows spaced 13 mm apart. On sashing strips, outline-quilt 6 mm from seam lines, using green thread. To bind the quilt, cut bias strips of dark green fabric 12.5 cm wide. Piece the strips to a length sufficient to go around the quilt. Fold the strip in half lengthways, turn under raw edges and sew over edges of quilt.

Cut narrow grosgrain ribbon into 18 cm lengths and tie each piece into a small bow. Stitch a bow to each bear. Sew wider red ribbon bows to sashing strips.

𝒫yramid 𝒬uilt

𝒻or this quilt design you can really clean out the remnant cupboard. Its charm relies on the myriad of colours and patterns randomly placed to make it a real patchwork quilt. After piecing the top and putting together the layers, quilt each pyramid shape 6 mm inside the seamline.

FINISHED SIZE: approx. 228 cm square.
NOTE: To make this quilt you need 561 pyramids and 34 half pyramids from assorted print fabrics. (50 cm of 115 cm-wide fabric yields 51 pyramids.) After cutting borders from brown and rust prints you will have excess fabric from which to cut more pyramids. When sewing use 6 mm seams.

Materials

A total of about 5 m of 115 cm-wide fabric scraps for pyramids; 90 cm-wide cotton fabric (2 m rust print and 2.3 m brown print) for borders; 4.6 m of 115 cm-wide fabric for backing; 228 cm square of polyester wadding; thread.

Instructions

Enlarge pyramid shape from diagram and make a template. Cut pyramids and half pyramids from various fabrics adding

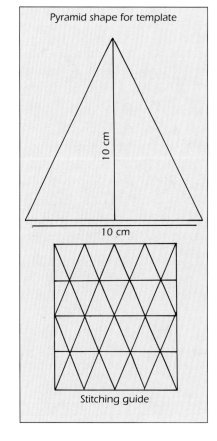

Pyramid shape for template

10 cm

10 cm

Stitching guide

6 mm all around template edges for seam allowances. After determining a colour sequence for pyramids, join them in rows following stitching guide. Each row has 33 pyramids and two half pyramids. Make 17 rows. Stitch rows together.

For borders, cut two 14 x 70 cm strips and two 14 x 195 cm strips from rust fabric. Stitch short strips to side edges of quilt top then stitch long strips along top and bottom edges. Cut two 17 x 195 cm strips and two 17 x 228 cm strips from brown fabric. Stitch to rust border as above. Piece fabric for quilt backing, assemble layers then quilt, referring to colour picture. Machine quilt or hand quilt the pyramids first, then diagonally quilt the rust border and channel-quilt (parallel lines) the brown border. Finish quilt according to instructions for *Blazing Star Beauty* (see page 26).

ℛOBBING 𝒫ETER TO 𝒫AY 𝒫AUL 𝒬UILT

𝒲hile this quilt is not one for the beginner, working with the same curved shapes continuously will help you to quickly master the techniques used. Each block consists of five parts, with the blue pieces being appliquéd onto the printed fabric. A very time-consuming but ultimately rewarding project.

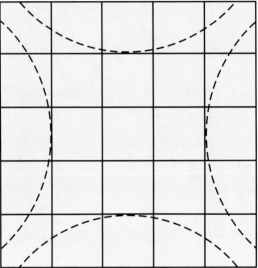

1 square = 2.5 cm

FINISHED SIZE: approx. 200 x 180 cm.
NOTE: The quilt pictured consists of 195 13 cm blocks with alternating blue and print centres. The blocks are arranged in 15 rows of 13 blocks each and the blue border strips are 9 cm wide.

Materials
4 m of 115 cm-wide blue cotton fabric; 3 m of cotton print fabric; 4 m of 115 cm-wide cotton backing fabric; 4.1 m of 90 cm-wide wadding; 8.2 m of bias binding.

Instructions
Cut two 188 x 9 cm strips and two 213 x 9 cm strips in blue fabric for borders. Make templates for centre shape and curved edge piece (see diagram). Adding 6 mm seam allowance on all sides, trace and cut the pattern pieces as follows: 98 blue centres and 97 light print centres; plus 388 blue curved edge pieces and 392 light print edge pieces. Clip curves and baste under seam allowances on all blue shapes, both centres and edge pieces. Pin blue curved edge pieces onto a light print centre, then appliqué the blue shapes to the print with tiny slip-stitches. Repeat to make 97 blocks. Then appliqué blue centres onto print edges to make 98 blocks.

Alternating between blue and print centres, assemble blocks in 15 horizontal rows of 13 blocks each. Add 9 cm-wide border strips to the sides first and then top and bottom of quilt to form a border. Trim strips to length required.

Cut and piece backing fabric to quilt size. Cut a same-size piece of wadding and sandwich between backing fabric and quilt top; quilt as desired. Finish raw edges with bias binding.

QUICK SQUARE COT QUILT

If you want to make a cot quilt easily and without too much fuss, then this is the pattern for you. It makes an ideal gift. Cut all your squares before you start sewing; using a rotary cutter and cutting mat will make this job even faster.

FINISHED SIZE: approx. 120 x 80 cm.
NOTE: 6 mm seams are used.

Materials

Same-weight 115 cm-wide cotton fabrics in the following: 2.2 m of yellow; 60 cm of pink; 20 cm of orange; 10 cm of red; 1 m of 150 cm-wide polyester wadding; 2 m of 50 mm-wide yellow binding.

Instructions

Cut an 8.7 cm-square template from heavy cardboard. Use this to trace 84 squares onto yellow fabric and cut out. Cut another 72 squares from pink fabric, 24 from orange and 12 from red. Separate the squares into twelve piles of 16 squares each containing one red, two orange, six pink and seven yellow. Take one pile and sew squares together with right sides facing in four rows of four by following diagram to form a square of 16 coloured squares. Repeat for remaining 11 piles.

   Cut three of the finished squares in half along the diagonal. Cut another into quarters along the diagonal. Join

patchwork squares together with right sides facing following diagram and taking care to keep pattern placement consistent. Cut wadding to size; pin, then baste it to wrong side. With right sides facing, stitch front to 98 x 146 cm yellow backing along lower edge and sides; trim. Turn through. Baste through three layers 15 mm inside edges formed by red,

orange and pink cross. Machine quilt along these lines in yellow cotton. Cut binding into two 98 cm lengths and stitch binding together along one long side and one end with right sides facing. Matching raw edges and with right sides facing, stitch one long edge to top of quilt front. Turn remaining raw edge under and slip-stitch.

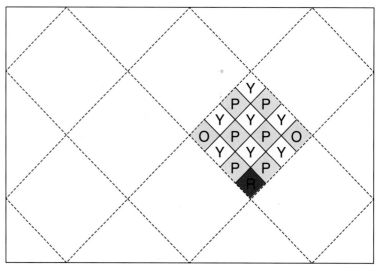

Assembly diagram
R = red
O = orange
Y = yellow
P = pink

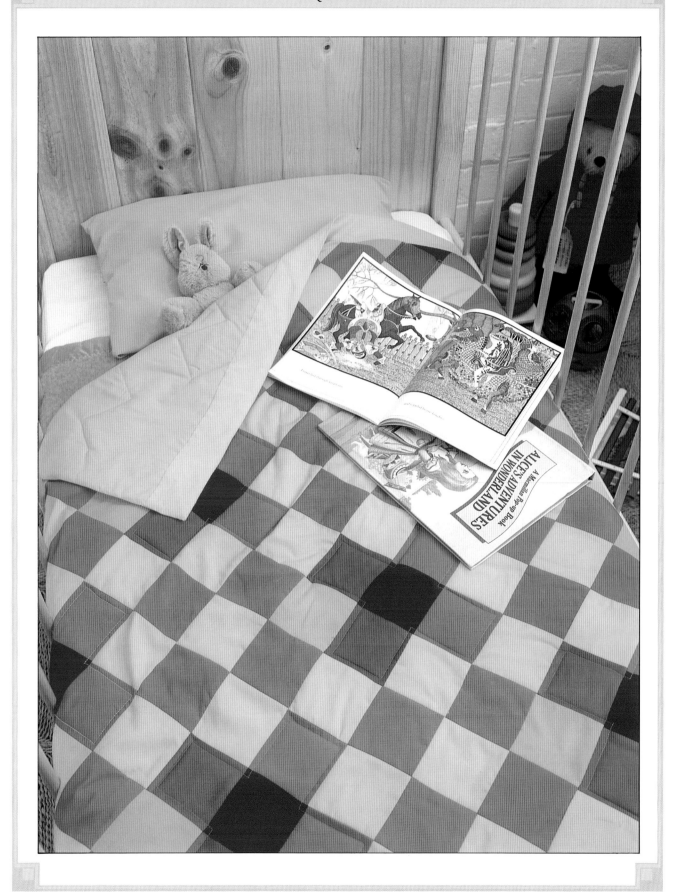

Country Nine Patch

At first glance, this quilt looks very old, but in fact it was only made a few years ago. The secret is the fabric choice, the simple yet very traditional patchwork pattern and quilting lines. Tiny floral prints, mini checks and polka-dot fabrics in country colours of rust, black, french blue, and olive green help give the antique look. This quilt has been hand quilted using easy-to-stitch diagonal lines, however you may choose a more intricate pattern.

FINISHED SIZE: approx. 200 x 173 cm.

NOTE: This traditional quilt consists of 12 cm-square nine-patch blocks and plain blocks arranged diagonally in rows (as diagram). The rows are framed with narrow inner and wide outer borders and the outer borders are bound in contrasting fabric. When planning your quilt, refer to the picture for colour and placement suggestions. Use 6 mm seams; pre-shrink fabric.

Materials

All metreage is from 115 cm-wide fabrics: 1.6 m of dark pindotted fabric (solid squares); 1 m each of assorted light and dark fabric scraps (nine-patch blocks); 1.7 m of light-coloured fabric (inner border); 2.10 m of dark-coloured fabric (outer border); 4 m of backing fabric; 200 x 173 cm wadding; 50 cm of dark fabric or 7.5 m of wide bias binding; cardboard or plastic (for templates); sewing and/or quilting thread; water-erasable marking pen; quilting frame or hoop (if desired).

Assembly diagram

Instructions

To cut the blocks: Make a 13.2 cm-square template (measurement includes 6 mm seam allowance). Cut 56 squares from dark pindotted fabric. Cut a 12 cm-square template in half diagonally for edging triangles. Add seam allowances to one triangle; set the other triangle aside. Cut 30 triangles from dark pindotted fabric (cut short sides of triangle with the straight of the grain). Set pieces aside.

Each nine-patch block has four dark-coloured and five light-coloured squares. Cut a 5.2 cm-square template (measurement includes seam allowance). Cut 288 squares from dark fabrics, 360 squares from light fabrics.

To piece blocks: Sew a strip of three squares (light, dark, light). Sew another strip of three (dark, light, dark). Sew a third strip the same as the first. Piece the three strips together to make a chequerboard pattern. Repeat for 72 blocks.

To assemble: Working diagonally from one corner, piece squares into strips following quilt assembly diagram. Join large triangle pieces to edge of strips as shown. Join strips into rows. Sew small corner triangles in place.

For inner border, cut two 138 x 6 cm and two 165 x 6 cm strips; piece if necessary. Join the shorter strips to the top and bottom of the pieced top. Join the longer strips to the sides.

For outer border, cut two 150 x 22 cm and two 205 x 17 cm strips; piece if necessary. Join to edges of inner border as shown on diagram.

Piece the backing fabric to fit the quilt top. Layer backing, wadding and pieced top. Pin then baste the layers together in a sunburst pattern (see page 101) then quilt as desired. Bind the edges with dark fabric or bias binding and slip-stitch to wrong side of quilt.

$\mathcal{E}$MBROIDERED $\mathcal{F}$AN $\mathcal{Q}$UILT

$\mathcal{C}$apture the opulence of the Victorian era by making this embroidered fan quilt. Rich silk and satin fabrics are appliquéd onto a background square. The seams are then heavily embroidered using pearl threads, or you may use silk threads.

FINISHED SIZE: 172 x 135 cm.
NOTE: All patterns and measurements for patterns and borders include a 6 mm seam allowance.

Materials

2.8 m of 115 cm-wide black taffeta fabric; 4 m of 115 cm-wide red satin for borders and quilt back; assorted scraps (totalling about 4 m) of silk, satin, taffeta (old neckties can be good sources of scraps); 3.6 m of flannel (or similar weight for wadding); assorted colours of stranded and pearl embroidery thread; tracing paper; firm cardboard or plastic for templates.

Instructions

Trace patterns and make templates using the full-size pattern pieces. Solid lines are cutting lines and dashed lines denote stitching line. Make a 21.2 cm square template for quilt blocks.

Using black taffeta fabric, cut 48 background squares and 48 fan centres. Cut seven wedges for each block (total of 336), using the fan wedge pattern, from silk, satin and taffeta fabric scraps. Cut two 160 x 11.2 cm borders and two 141.2 x 11.2 cm borders from red satin fabric. Leave remaining fabric for quilt back.

To make one block
With right sides together, matching points A and B, fold one fan wedge in half lengthwise. Stitch from fold to the AB point, taking a 6 mm seam allowance. Turn the tip right side out, forming the pointed wedge tip. Repeat for

remaining fan wedges.
Stitch seven prepared wedges together along the sides to form a fan. Pin the fan to a black taffeta square. Baste under the curved edge of a fan centre piece. Pin the fan centre in the corner of a square, adjusting the position of the fan so the fan centre covers the bottom raw edges of the fan wedges.

Baste the side edges of the fan to the black square just outside the seam line. Appliqué the curved edge of the fan centre; remove the basting along this edge.

Embellish the seams between the wedges with a variety of embroidery stitches (such as buttonhole, feather-stitch, stem and chain, see page 103), working in assorted colours and threads. Add simple motifs in the fan centres, if desired (use picture as a guide).

To make quilt top
Make 48 fan blocks. Referring to

colour picture lay out the blocks in six rows with eight blocks in each row. The fans in the quilt shown form a circle in the quilt centre, surrounded by partial circles. Join the blocks into rows, then stitch the rows together. Add decorative embroidery stitches along the block seamlines.

Stitch the longer border strips to the sides of the quilt; trim excess seams. Stitch remaining borders to the top and bottom of quilt; trim seams. Add decorative embroidery stitches

along the border seams and simple motifs at the border corners, if desired.

To complete quilt
Piece red satin backing fabric into a rectangle about 2.5 cm bigger on all sides than the quilt top. To make backing, cut length of fabric the length of the quilt and join fabric strips to either side of centre piece. Piece flannel together the same size as quilt back.

Lay flannel rectangle on the floor. Centre quilt back on

flannel with right side of the quilt back up. Centre quilt top wrong side up over quilt back. Pin layers together around outer edges.

Stitch around the edges of quilt top, leaving an opening to turn through. Trim seams, clip corners and turn quilt through to the right side. Slip-stitch opening closed.

Tie the quilt top to the quilt back at all the block corners, forming the knots on the quilt back (see page 103).

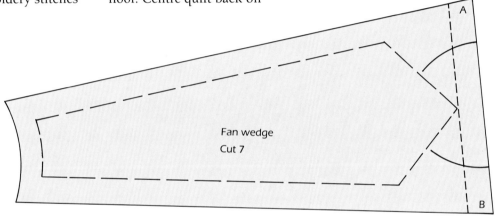

Fan wedge
Cut 7

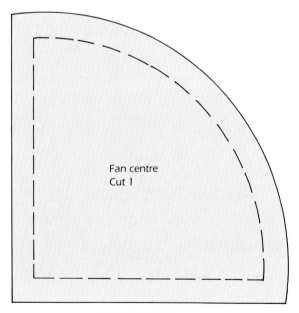

Fan centre
Cut 1

Full-size patterns

Wallhangings

If you're a little hesitant about embarking on a quilt, why not start with a wallhanging? It's a good way to experiment with colour and shapes and patchwork wallhangings make delightful wall decorations.

FRAMED FOLDED PATCHWORK PICTURE

Framing your patchwork is one of the most decorative ways of
presenting it. For this piece of Thai folded patchwork,
shades of one colour have been selected.

Materials

20 cm each of seven 90 cm
wide fabrics in different
shades of blue; 30 cm square
of calico.

Instructions

Work wallhanging following
general instructions for
folded patchwork block on
page 47, to give a 30 cm
patchwork piece. Instead of
cutting the strips for the
folded pieces 3 cm wide, we
cut ours 2.5 cm wide and
overlapped each piece for
5 mm instead of 7 mm for
each layer.

When patchwork is
complete and border is
worked, baste raw edges of
border and calico together to
hold firmly so work may be
framed. Frame as desired.

HOW TO MAKE A FOLDED PATCHWORK BLOCK

Cut a calico backing square the size of the finished block, adding 5 mm seam allowance all around. Mark the centre by folding in quarters diagonally and pressing. Where the lines intersect is the exact centre. Cut a small square of fabric for the centre and baste onto the calico, centring it exactly.

Cut 2.5 cm-wide strips of fabric. Fold in half lengthwise with wrong sides together and press. With all raw edges even, pin the strip along one edge of the centre square. Machine-stitch through all layers 5 mm from the raw edge. Trim the strip to the length of the square.

Continue adding strips around each edge in a clockwise direction, building up the layers in a log cabin design and changing colours as desired. Each round should overlap the previous round by about 7 mm. (This can be varied.)

Continue until four rounds are completed. Then to make the triangular layer cut enough 3.5 cm fabric squares to fit around the edge of the round. Fold each small square in half, then quarters, and press. Pin folded squares so that the folded point meets the folded edge of the previous strip, as shown. Pin a complete round of folded squares, overlapping each one over the previous one. Stitch in position.

Continue adding strips until about 6 cm of the calico block is left uncovered. If at this stage any strips are lifting up and showing the stitching lines, they can be slip-stitched down to keep them flat.

Cut a 6 cm-wide strip of border fabric and stitch around the edge of the patchwork strips, continuing the log cabin design.

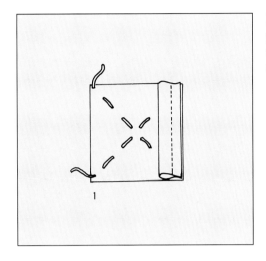

Baste centre square in place, fold the first strip in half and stitch to one side of the square.

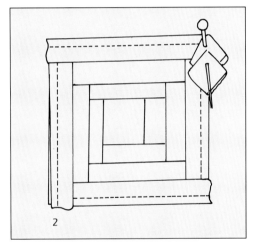

Fold fabric square in half then half again, laying the raw edges against the raw edges of the previous strip, and overlapping each triangle.

Now your block is ready for use as a potholder, pockets on a carry bag, cushion cover, apron bib, placemats (make them a rectangular shape), jacket pockets or framed for your own handmade artwork.

Arrow Log Cabin Wallhanging

The arrow log cabin design is achieved through careful placement of light and dark fabric strips. Once the log cabin blocks are constructed some of the blocks are turned to create the arrow effect. Quick and easy to construct, the wallhanging can be made by hand or machine.

FINISHED SIZE: approx. 90 x 70 cm.
NOTE: 6 mm seams used throughout.

Materials
Scraps of print fabrics in light and dark colours; 10 cm of 115 cm-wide black cotton fabric; 60 cm of 115 cm-wide print fabric (borders); 70 cm of 90 cm-wide polyester wadding; 1.4 m of 115 cm-wide calico.

Instructions
Cut 24 each of 4.2 cm squares in black fabric for centres and 13.2 cm squares in calico. Cut 2.7 cm-wide light and dark fabric strips for logs.

Following our instructions for working log cabin on page 25, piece blocks with three rounds of logs. Begin with a dark centre and piece squares starting with two light, followed by two dark for each round. Make 24 blocks. Then join to make four rows of six blocks and join rows together.

Cut two 67 x 10 cm rectangles for top and bottom borders and two 73 x 10 cm rectangles for side borders. With raw edges even and right sides together, stitch side borders to quilt. Repeat for top and bottom borders of quilt. Cut wadding to size of quilt top and backing fabric to same size. Layer quilt top, wadding and backing fabric. Baste in a sunburst pattern (see page 101) and quilt as desired.

Cut 5 cm-wide strips of border fabric and piece to measure 3.3 m.

With wrong sides together press binding in half. With all raw edges even, stitch right sides of quilt and binding together. Turn binding to back of quilt and slip-stitch in place.

Lone Star Wallhanging

A piece with a real country feel, the lone star patch often called the Ohio or Texas star is the focal point of this wallhanging. Floral and plain cottons combine with a calico background to form the star blocks. To highlight the hand quilting the stitching is worked in a contrasting thread.

FINISHED SIZE:
approx. 90 cm square.
NOTE: Seam allowance
6 mm.

Materials

50 cm of 112 cm-wide cream homespun;
50 cm of 112 cm-wide burgundy homespun;
30 cm of 90 cm-wide spotted cotton fabric;
10 cm each of four 90 cm-wide assorted cotton fabrics for blocks; 90 cm square of cotton backing fabric;
90 cm square of polyester wadding.

Instructions

Cut cream fabric as follows. For borders: two 67 x 6.5 cm strips; two 78 x 6.5 cm strips. For blocks: eight 9.2 cm squares; twenty 8 cm squares cut in half to make 40 triangles.

Cut burgundy fabric as follows. For borders: two 78 x 10 cm strips; two 95 x 10 cm strips; one 9.2 cm square; four 8 cm squares cut in half to make eight triangles. Tabs: cut one 40 x 10 cm strip.

Cut spotted fabric into two 25.2 cm squares, cut in half to make four triangles; one 26.4 cm square, cut in quarters to make four triangles.

From each of four different fabrics, cut four 9.2 cm squares and four 8 cm squares (cut in half to make eight triangles).
Blocks: Lay out squares and small triangles for blocks. Working from Diagram 1, and matching corners carefully, pin and stitch small triangles together to make squares. Press all seams to one side. Stitch squares together to make a row. Stitch rows into a block. Press. Make five blocks. Lay blocks on flat surface. Place dominant block in centre. Working from Diagram 2, stitch two blocks to either side of central block. Stitch small triangles to either end of three-block strip. Press. Stitch large triangles to either side of remaining blocks. Press. Stitch one-block strip to either side of three-block strip. Stitch small triangles to remaining corners, press. *Borders:* pin and stitch shortest cream strips to sides, press. Stitch remaining cream strips to top and bottom. Repeat for

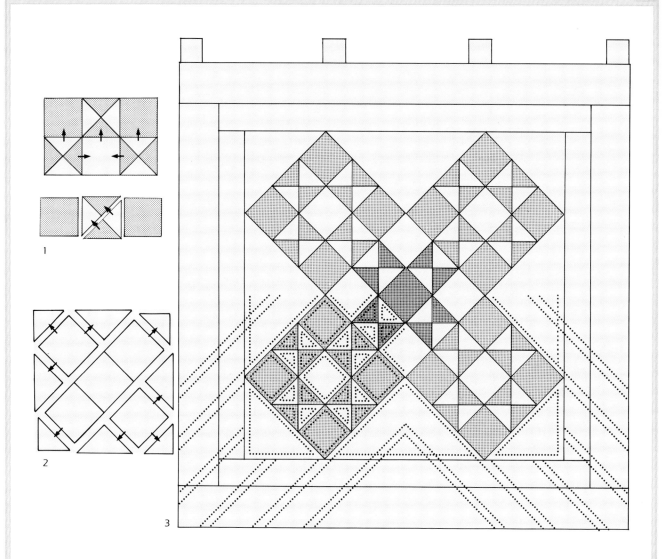

1

2

3

burgundy border, stitching sides first. Press.

Quilting: Sandwich wadding between wrong sides of backing and front. Starting from the centre, tack the three layers together in a sunburst pattern (see page 101), smoothing fabric as you go. Tacking lines should be no more than 15 cm apart.

Quilting is simply a tiny running-stitch. Using quilting thread, begin with a knot. Insert needle from the bottom through all three layers. Gently pull the knot from underneath until the knot slips through the bottom layer and stays in the wadding. With one hand on top and one underneath, make a small back-stitch, then push the needle straight up through all three layers. Try for about four stitches on the needle as you quilt. To end a line of quilting, make a couple of small back-stitches, run the needle through the wadding for a short distance and cut the thread. Always start with a block in the middle and work out. Quilt around all squares and triangles 6 mm in from edge. Following quilting lines from blocks, quilt borders in straight lines (see Diagram 3)

Binding: Trim backing and wadding 2 cm smaller than front. Turn under seam allowance on front and turn to back. Pin in place. Handstitch securely. For tabs, fold remaining burgundy strip, fold in half lengthwise, with right sides together, stitch. Press and turn through and cut strip into four. Fold each strip in half and overlock edges; pin and stitch to top of wallhanging, placing the four tabs equal distance apart.

HOMES ON THE HILL WALLHANGING

This framed scene sports handy dowel pegs to hang hats, keys, or even matching oven mitts. Store-bought toy farmyard animals give the scene a naive look, and make the picture three-dimensional. Great for the kitchen, it would also be very handy positioned near the front or back door of your home.

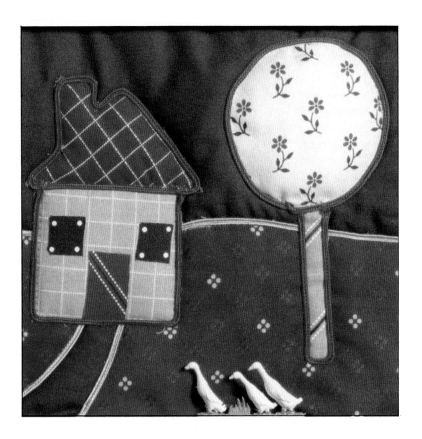

Materials

56 x 25 cm rectangle of navy blue cotton for picture background; scraps of various burgundy, beige and white prints for picture details; narrow braids in burgundy and biscuit; 40 cm of 120 cm-wide polyester wadding; polyester fibrefill; fusible hemming tape; farmyard animals (from toy shops). Frame: 70 x 12 mm and 42 x 12 mm maple; 13 mm particle board; 6 mm dowel pegs; glue; nails.

Instructions

Frame
Finished size of frame is approx. 600 x 320 mm. For frame front, cut two sides 320 mm long and one top 520 mm long from 42 mm maple. For deeper bottom piece, cut 70 mm maple 520 mm long. Using simple butt-joints, glue and nail frame together. Drill five 6 mm holes in bottom frame piece; glue 60 mm-long dowel pegs in place. Glue frame to backing board, cut to size from 13 mm particle board. Finish with two coats of clear acrylic.

Picture
Enlarge pattern by drawing a new grid on a large sheet of paper following scale marked. Your grid should have the same

Homes on the Hill Wallhanging
  (cont'd)

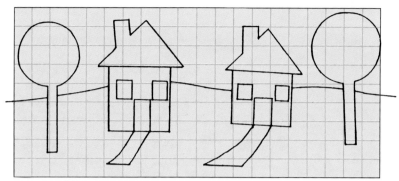

1 square = 2.5 cm

number of squares as the original drawing. Carefully copy the design onto your enlarged grid, then go over it with a felt-tipped pen. Copy individual motifs for houses, trees and hillside onto tracing paper and cut out to use as patterns. No seams are needed. Cut out pieces from appropriate fabrics, using the photograph as a guide.

Lay background fabric out and mark a 2 cm border inside edges (this will be turned to the back when the picture is finished). Pin fabric motifs in place, as Step 1. When satisfied with positioning, remove houses and use fusible hemming tape to iron windows and doors into place, as Step 2. Cut two layers of polyester wadding 52 x 21 cm. Position picture over wadding and pin. Machine motifs in place using zigzag stitch, leaving small openings at the bases of the tree tops. Use a knitting needle to push polyester fibrefill into tree top through opening, as Step 3. Topstitch braid around raw edges on main pieces, covering zigzag stitches, as Step 4. When picture is complete, turn border edges to back of work and handsew to secure, as Step 5. Handsew farmyard animals in place and fix picture into frame with craft glue or double-sided tape. To keep clean, it's a good idea to spray picture with a fabric protector.

Step 1. Pinning motifs in place

Step 2. Ironing on windows

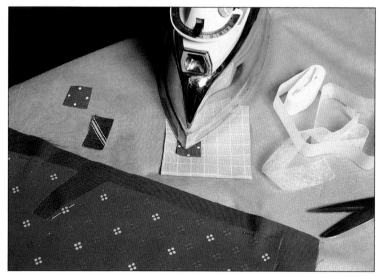

Step 3. Padding tree tops

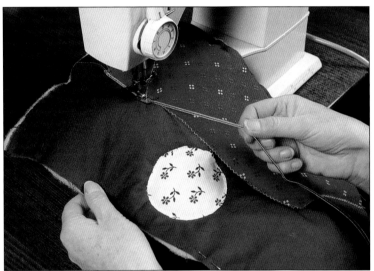

Step 4. Topstitching braid

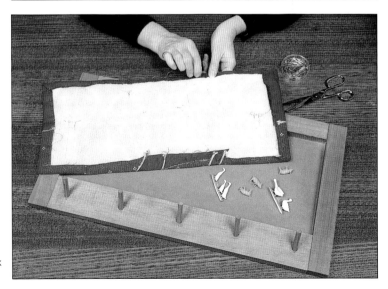

Step 5. Sewing edges to back

Cushions

Cushions are an ideal project for the patchwork beginner as they can be made quickly. You can start off with traditional designs, making them either by hand or machine, and practise your quilting technique on them as well. We've included instructions on piping and making your own fabric frills. And we show you how to make covers that are easily removed without the use of a zipper. Remember to use good quality cotton fabrics as cushions require frequent laundering to keep them fresh.

$\mathcal{L}$OG $\mathcal{C}$ABIN $\mathcal{C}$USHIONS

$\mathcal{O}$ne of the most popular and best known patchwork patterns is Log Cabin. Choose scraps of textured cream cotton fabrics to make this matching trio of cushions. They have a back lap closing and the whole cushion, including the quilting, can be made on the sewing machine.

FINISHED SIZE: 45 cm square.
NOTE: 6 mm seam allowance used.

Materials

For one cushion.
Two 15 cm squares of two cream fabrics, 6.2 cm wide strips of various fabrics at least 45 cm long, 15 cm square of fusible interfacing, 90 cm of 115 cm wide calico, and a 45 cm square cushion insert.

Instructions

Pre-wash all fabrics to avoid shrinkage. Fuse interfacing to wrong side of one 15 cm square of fabric. Cut heart shape (see page 106) from this bonded fabric piece and using a close zigzag, stitch heart to remaining fabric square. With right sides facing, sew a strip of fabric to the centre square. Do not pre-cut fabric strips but cut away excess after stitching to make strip same size as centre square. (See page 25 for photographs showing log cabin block.) Press seam allowance away from centre. Rotating centre square, continue to stitch strips of fabric to remaining edges of centre square. Continue in this manner until you have three strips attached on all four sides (total of 12 strips).

Cut a 46.2 cm square of calico. With wrong sides together pin patched piece to calico backing. Using a long machine stitch machine quilt the layers together, stitching close to the seams from the right side of the patched piece. Cut two 46.2 x 57.7 cm rectangles for cushion-backs. Hem one long edge on each piece. With right sides facing cushion-front, overlap hemmed edges of cushion-backs until they are the same size as the front piece. Stitch backs to front rounding corners slightly. Trim seams, turn through and press.

FOLDED PATCHWORK CUSHIONS

The hill tribes of Thailand use a form of patching called folded patchwork. This clever technique requires the fabric pieces to be folded before they are stitched in place. Each layer overlaps the previous layer with one row being a row of decorative triangles. Bright contrasting colours work well with this technique.

FINISHED SIZE: approx 40 cm square.

Materials

60 cm of 90 cm-wide navy cotton fabric; 20 cm each of five 90 cm-wide cotton fabrics in rust, blue and prints of these colours; 40 cm square of calico; 30 cm zip; 40 cm cushion insert.

Instructions

Make cushion front panel following general instructions for folded patchwork block on page 47. Add two outer borders instead of one. The first border is cut 5 cm wide and the second is 10 cm wide. Your finished cushion front should measure approximately 40 cm square.

Cut two 40 x 21.5 cm rectangles in navy cotton. With right sides together, and using a 1.5 cm seam, stitch in each end approximately 5 cm. Open out, press seam allowance under on centre opening. Insert zip. Pin front of cushion to back with right sides facing, leaving zip open a little. Stitch around cushion, rounding corners as you go. Trim and overlock or zigzag the seam. Turn through and fill with the cushion insert.

ℱOUR ℭUSHIONS WITH ℳATCHING 𝒲ALLHANGING

ℋovering Hawks, Crosses and Losses, Jacob's Ladder and Beggar's Block are the patterns used in these cushions and wallhanging. You can make good use of fabric remainders by choosing a variety of colourful cottage prints to make these self-piped or frilled cushions.

CUSHIONS

FINISHED SIZE: 30 cm square; frill is 9 cm wide.
NOTE: 6 mm seam allowance used.

Materials

For one cushion (there are four different designs).

Scraps of cotton fabrics for patchwork blocks; 35 cm of 115 cm-wide fabric for frill; 30 cm of 115 cm-wide fabric for piping; 1.3 m cord of desired thickness for piping; 40 cm of 115 cm-wide fabric for cushion back; cardboard; quarter seamer; cushion inserts.

Instructions

Draw a 30 cm square on a piece of cardboard. Draw up pattern on cardboard, following pattern diagram. Cut along lines to make a cardboard template of each pattern piece. Mark out template shape on fabric, using a soft lead pencil or a water-soluble marker. Using quarter seamer, add 6 mm seam allowance to each pattern piece before cutting out. Piece blocks in segments, either by hand or machine. Press seams towards darker fabric to avoid seam shadow on right side.

Frill
Join fabric as necessary to form a 240 x 10.5 cm-wide strip for frill. With right sides facing, stitch short ends together. Narrowly hem one long edge.

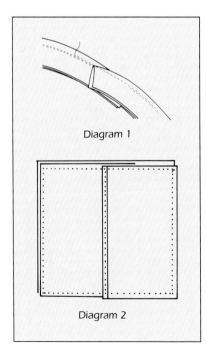

Diagram 1

Diagram 2

Stitch two gathering threads along the other long edge. Pull up threads, gathering frill to fit cushion front. With right sides together and raw edges even, stitch frill to cushion front.

Piping
Follow general instructions to prepare piping (see page 102). Pin piping to right side of cushion front, with piping stitch line just inside the seam line. Allow ends to overlap. Undo a few stitches of piping seam and trim cord. Overlap ends and stitch piping in place (see diagram 1).

Cushion back (lapped style)
Cut two 31.2 x 20 cm rectangles of fabric. Hem one long edge on each piece. With right sides facing cushion-front, overlap hemmed edges of cushion-backs until they are the same size as the front piece (see diagram 2). Stitch backs to front, rounding corners slightly. Trim seams, turn through and press.

Four Cushions with Matching
Wallhanging (cont'd)

WALLHANGING

FINISHED SIZE: 43 cm square.
NOTE: 6 mm seam allowance
used.

Materials
Scraps of cotton fabrics for
patchwork blocks; 1 m of
90 cm-wide cotton homespun
fabric; 44 cm square of wadding.

Instructions
Working in half scale, make up
four patchwork blocks as for
Patchwork Cushions.

Border
Using scraps, cut 64 border
triangles from small triangle on
Hovering Hawks block, omitting
seam allowance. Cut two 17 x
4 cm joining strips and one 32 x

BEGGAR'S BLOCK

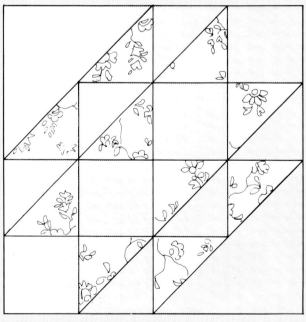

HOVERING HAWKS

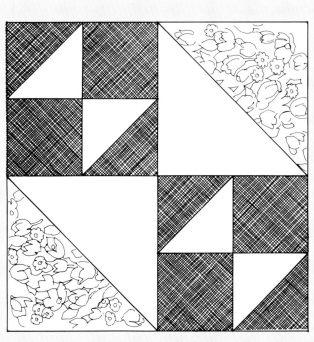

CROSSES AND LOSSES

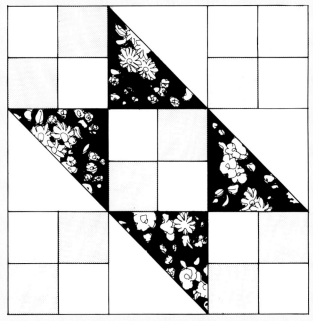

JACOB'S LADDER

4 cm strip from homespun. With right sides facing and using short strips, stitch two patchwork blocks together, then stitch all four blocks together using the long strip and trimming ends as necessary.

Cut two 34 x 6.2 cm and two 44 x 6.2 cm strips from homespun fabric. Stitch short strips to top and bottom of patchwork, trimming ends as necessary. Stitch long strips to sides of patchwork. Press seam allowance to wrong side of fabric on border triangles. Using picture as a guide, slip-stitch triangles in place. Cut four triangles half the size of each corner square and work as for border triangles. Press finished work.

Backing
Cut two 44 cm-square pieces of backing fabric. Sandwich wadding between patchwork and one backing piece. Pin and tack in a sunburst pattern (see page 101). Quilt as desired. With right sides facing, stitch second backing piece to quilted piece, leaving a small opening to turn through. To avoid flattening wadding, do not press. Slip-stitch opening closed. Make two hanging loops and slip-stitch in place.

Kitchen Ideas

The colour and homeliness of patchwork make it perfect for the kitchen. Tablecloths, napkins, tea cosies and placemats can all be made with patchwork and will add brightness to any kitchen.

65

LACE-EDGED PATCHWORK CLOTH

This bright and cheery tablecloth makes a delightful breakfast or outdoor cloth. Easy to make as the squares aren't too small, it is a great way of using your fabric scraps. When working with the one shape you'll save lots of time and pieces will join together easily if you make a template first.

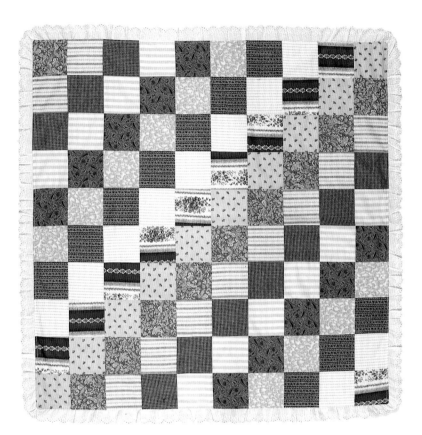

FINISHED SIZE: 100 cm square (excluding frill).
NOTE: 6 mm seam allowance used.

Materials

1 m of 115 cm-wide fabric for backing; 4.10 m of 4 cm-wide pre-gathered broderie anglaise; scraps of desired fabrics.

Instructions

Cut an 11.2 cm-square template from cardboard and cut 100 squares of fabric using your template as a pattern. To form rows, sew squares together in random colour and pattern sequences pressing each seam. Then join rows. With raw edges together and right sides facing, stitch broderie anglaise to cloth. Pin backing to cloth with right sides facing and leaving a 30 cm opening on one edge for turning. Turn through, slip-stitch opening closed. Press cloth and topstitch 6 mm from fabric edge.

Patchwork Potholders and Appliqued Tea Towels

These look great when stitched as a co-ordinating pair—use one of the potholder fabrics for the tea towels. They make a wonderful gift for a kitchen tea or as a house-warming present.

PATCHWORK POTHOLDERS

FINISHED SIZE: 20 cm square.
NOTE: 1 cm seam allowance used.

Materials

Scraps of fabric to make patches; two 20 cm squares of wadding; 22 cm square of fabric for backing.

Instructions

Cut an 8 cm-square template from cardboard and cut four squares from one fabric and five from the other. Piece into rows of three, pressing seams as you go. Join rows, matching seams. Place patchwork right side up, on top of both pieces of wadding and centre these on wrong side of backing fabric, baste together. Machine quilt through all layers at seams. Fold 1 cm of raw edge of backing to wrong side then fold over again to right side of patchwork to form a binding. Stitch in place.

APPLIQUÉD TEA TOWELS

Materials

For one tea towel.
Purchased tea towel; 20 cm

square of fabric and fusible interfacing; small contrasting fabric scrap for geese feet and beaks.

Instructions

Fuse interfacing to wrong side of fabric. Enlarge pattern and cut geese from fabric. Baste in position and using a small close zigzag, stitch in position on raw edges following design lines.

1 square = 2.5 cm

Cottage Tea Cosy

This English thatched cottage tea cosy can be made using purchased floral appliqués and quilted fabric to save time, or you may choose to quilt your own design and hand-embroider the gardens.

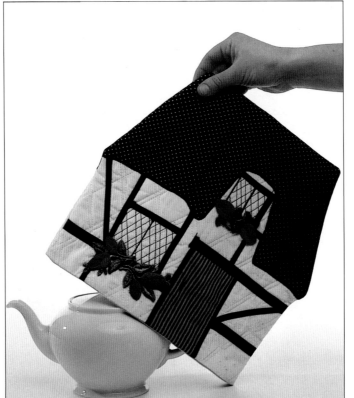

Materials

0.5 m of pre-quilted fabric (or enough to quilt your own); 0.5 m of calico for lining; 0.3 m of polka-dot fabric; scrap of brown striped fabric; 2 m of brown bias tape; purchased floral appliqués; two 40 cm squares of wadding.

Instructions

Enlarge pattern adding 6 mm seam allowances to outside edges. Cut two cottage shapes from quilted fabric, two from calico and two from wadding. Cut two rooftops from polka-dot fabric and a door from striped fabric. Mark stitching lines for bias tape 'timberwork' using tailor's chalk or small running stitches. With wrong sides facing, tack wadding to cottage front and back. Stitch bias tape to front of cottage incorporating door beneath tape as you work. Machine-stitch doorknob, and 'panes' of windows. Attach floral appliqués.

Tack one roof to each cottage piece. Stitch along 'eaves' using close satin-stitch to secure.

With right sides facing, stitch front to back leaving bottom open. Turn out.

With right sides facing, stitch calico lining together leaving bottom open and an opening at top for turning through. With wrong side out, place the lining over cosy, lining the seams up. Stitch around the bottom of the cosy. Push cosy through lining opening to inside and slip-stitch to close.

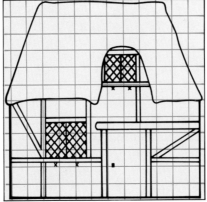

1 square = 2.5 cm

Pastel Tea Cosy

Satin scraps are used to make this pretty pastel tea cosy which has ribbon
trimming the seams and satin cording over the curved edge. To top
it off a delicate silken tassel hangs down from the centre.

FINISHED SIZE: width
45 cm, height 30 cm.
NOTE: 6 mm seam
allowance used.

Materials

Scraps of six satin
fabrics; 40 cm of
115 cm-wide fabric for
lining; 40 cm of five
6 mm-wide ribbons
and 1 m of 6 mm-wide
ribbon for binding
bottom edge; 80 cm of
three braids in different
widths; purchased silk
tassel; two 50 x 35 cm squares
of wadding; 1 m of fine cord.

Instructions

Using a 45 x 30 cm piece of
paper as a pattern, draw an oval
shaped semi-circle to fit on the
paper. From lining fabric, cut
two of this shape, adding 6 mm
seam allowance on all sides.

Divide the circle into six
equal-sized wedges. In the
centre from the bottom edge of
the paper draw a triangle 15 cm
wide with 15 cm sides (see
photograph). Cut templates of
all these pieces adding 6 mm
seam allowance to all sides of
templates and keeping original
pattern intact. Cut two of each
piece. With right sides facing,

stitch wedges together
to form front and
back. Stitch ribbons in
place over seamlines.
Trimming 3 mm from
seam allowance on
side edges of triangle,
stitch triangle in place
over wedges, making
sure bottom raw edges
are even. Stitch braids
in place making sure
that first braid is lying
over raw edges of
triangle, and mitring
ribbon at corner. With
right sides facing, sew front to
back along curved edge
including tassel in seam. Baste
one wadding piece to wrong
side of each lining piece. Stitch
together leaving bottom open.
Place lining inside cosy, binding
raw edges with ribbon.
Handstitch cord in place around
curved edge.

Nine Patch Kitchen Set

Always in fashion for kitchenware is the traditional colouring of blue and white. This co-ordinating nine patch kitchen set includes placemats, serviettes, potholders, and a butcher's apron with a special patched pocket.

Materials

2 m of 115 cm-wide dark print fabric; 1 m of 115 cm-wide light print fabric; 90 cm of 90 cm-wide calico; 60 cm of 90 cm-wide thin wadding. Four 22 cm squares of felt; 1.8 m of tape.

PLACEMATS
Makes four.
FINISHED SIZE: approx. 37 x 30 cm.
NOTE: 6 mm seams used throughout unless otherwise stated. Always press seams towards the darker fabrics to avoid shadows.

Cut nine A pieces for each placemat (five light and four dark or four light and five dark). Piece together in three strips of three, alternating lights

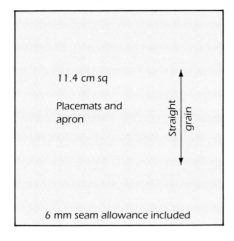

11.4 cm sq

Placemats and apron

Straight grain

6 mm seam allowance included

Potholder

6 mm seam allowance included

3.7 cm sq

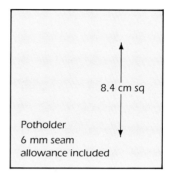

8.4 cm sq

Potholder

6 mm seam allowance included

Placemat border

6 mm seam allowance included

4.6 cm sq

and darks as pictured. Join the strips, matching seams.

Cut 18 B pieces for each placemat (eight light and 10 dark, or vice versa). Piece into two strips, alternating light and dark. Stitch each strip to two opposite edges of the placemat. Press seams towards dark pieces. Sandwich a 36 x 30 cm wadding piece between patched top and a same-size backing fabric (light print). Baste in a sunburst pattern, then quilt by machine along patchwork seams as desired. Repeat for remaining three placemats.

Cut out dark patches for potholder and apron, then use remainder of dark fabric to make a 3 cm-wide bias strip (see page 103). Press 7 mm under along one edge of bias. With raw edges together and right sides facing, pin, then stitch around placemat, over-lapping bias ends. Trim wadding. Fold bias over to back of placemat, pin along seam 'ditch', making sure bias at back is pinned in place. Stitch in the 'ditch' by machine.

NAPKINS
Cut four 40 cm squares of light floral fabric. Narrow-hem all sides.

POTHOLDERS
Makes two.
Cut eight C pieces (four light and four dark) and nine D pieces (four light and five dark or vice versa), for each potholder. Piece D squares together using same method as placemats, then piece the C pieces together, having D as the centre square.

Cut a same-size piece of light fabric for backing; sandwich felt square between the two layers, baste. Bind with bias as for placemats, adding a folded and stitched bias loop to hang potholder.

APRON
Cut calico apron piece according to diagram. Press 1 cm under all around then another 1 cm. Topstitch from right side around apron as desired.

Pocket
Cut nine A pieces (five light and four dark) and piece together as for placemats. Cut a same-size piece of calico and place it right sides together with patched

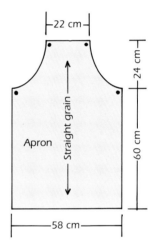

22 cm

24 cm

Apron

Straight grain

60 cm

58 cm

piece. Stitch around (1 cm from edge) leaving a 15 cm gap on one edge. Trim seams. Turn through, press allowance in and handstitch gap closed. Position pocket on apron as desired and topstitch in place on three sides.

For neck strap and waist ties, stitch 60 cm lengths of tape or stitched bias onto apron at large dots. Press.

Wearable Patchwork

Patched and quilted clothing was traditionally worn in countries with cold climates to keep the body warm. Today, patchwork clothing and accessories can be worn anywhere in any season of the year. When making patchwork clothing choose fabrics which are compatible in their care method and are of a similar weight. Use fine soft waddings to help avoid making a quilted garment too bulky. Pay particular attention to seam finishes, if they are not hidden in layers of fabric take the time to finish them properly to give your garments a professional look.

FLORAL PATCHED SHAWL

Look stylish while keeping warm in a patchwork wool wrap. Small amounts of wool challis remnant are ideal, or perhaps you have some fabric leftovers from your winter wardrobe. Choose your favourite winter tonings in a variety of print sizes for the best 'wrap' on beating the winter weather.

FINISHED SIZE: approx. 180 cm square.
NOTE: 6 mm seam allowance used.

Materials

Six patterned lightweight wool or wool challis fabrics, 115 cm wide in the following quantities: 0.6 m fabric A; 0.5 m fabric B; 0.5 m fabric C; 0.8 m fabric D; 0.7 m fabric E; 0.7 m fabric F; 3.6 m of 90 cm-wide winter cotton or lightweight wool for backing.

Instructions

Group fabrics together to determine a sequence for the shawl. Assign each fabric a letter (A, B, C, D, E, F) with A as the central one and the other letters radiating outwards.

Cut a 57 cm square from fabric A. Cut fabrics B and C into 10 cm-wide strips; fabrics D and E into 12.5 cm-wide strips; and F into 9 cm-wide strips.

Piece each together to form long strips.

From the B strip, cut two 57 cm-long strips and two 74.5 cm-long strips. With right sides facing, pin the two 57 cm strips to opposite sides of the central square. Use approx. 6 mm seams (you may have to make minor adjustments to seam allowances on outer strips). Pin and stitch remaining B strips to the other sides of the central square in the same way (see photograph). Cut remaining fabric strips as follows: C: two 74.5 cm strips; two 92 cm strips.
D: two 92 cm strips; two 114.5 cm strips.
E: two 114.5 cm strips; two 137 cm strips.
F: two 137 cm strips; two 152.5 cm strips.

Stitch strips to shawl in alphabetical order.

For the border, cut four 10 x 12.5 cm strips and four 12.5 cm squares from remaining A fabric and sixteen 12.5 cm lengths each from B, C, D, and F strips. Following the pattern in the photograph, with right sides facing, sew these lengths together on longest sides to form two 154.2 cm-long strips and two 176.8 cm-long strips. Attach as before to shawl.

Cut and piece backing fabric as required to make it the same size as the patched piece. With right sides facing sew backing to shawl leaving a 50 cm opening on one edge. Turn through and press, slip-stitch opening closed. Top-stitch the shawl 6 mm from the edge of the fabric.

Patchwork Swag Bag

Always a popular way of carrying your worldly possessions, this patched duffel is made from an interesting assortment of fabric shapes. The bag ends are made from wide fabric strips, while the distinctive centre band is made from pieced triangles.

Materials

Fabric scraps for patchwork; 1.5 m of 115 cm-wide cotton fabric for lining and bag base; 0.7 m of 150 cm-wide polyester wadding; 1.1 m of satin bias tape; eyelets; satin cord.

Instructions

Cut two 34 cm-diameter circles (see page 103) and a 107 x 64 cm rectangle from both cotton fabric and wadding. Patch fabric shapes together to form a same-sized rectangle which has a pieced triangular band in the centre (see photograph). Baste wadding to wrong side of corresponding patched pieces, working in a sunburst pattern (see page 101) toward edges. Quilt through both layers by machine or hand following patch seamlines. Join short edges of rectangle together with right sides facing and 1.5 cm seam allowances.

Cut a 50 x 12 cm strap from cotton. Fold in half lengthwise and stitch with 1 cm seams. Trim seams and turn through.

Centre on bag side seam with one end 20 cm from lower edge and the other 6 cm from top edge; stitch.

Attach circular base to patchwork body along lower edge with right sides facing and 1.5 cm seam allowance. Trim; turn through. Assemble lining in the same way, leaving an opening in base for turning through. With wrong side out, place lining over bag so that right sides are facing and stitch top edges together. Trim all seams and pull bag through lining. Slip-stitch opening closed. Bind mouth edge with bias tape. Punch eyelets at even intervals through all layers 3 cm below top edge. Thread cord through eyelets and knot ends together.

8 cm

8 cm

Cut as many as may be required for centre band

Centre Band Triangle
6 mm seam allowance included

7.2 cm

Folded Patchwork Apron

The traditional Thai method of folded patchwork looks great on the bib of this brightly coloured apron. The generous comfortable styling works well in protecting clothes from kitchen spills.

Materials
1 m of 115 cm-wide red cotton fabric; 20 cm of 90 cm-wide cotton fabric in each of the following colours: green, blue, grey, black and yellow; 23 cm square of calico; 23 cm square of red cotton fabric.

Instructions
Bib
Work a folded patchwork block (see page 47). Refer to photograph for fabric colours used. Finished size is 23 cm square. Baste red cotton square to back of finished patchwork with wrong sides facing.

Cut a 23 x 10 cm strip in red fabric. With right sides together machine stitch, using 1 cm seam, to one edge of patchwork square. Press and turn under a 1 cm seam allowance on the unstitched edge of the strip. Slip-stitch this edge to machine stitching on the wrong side of patchwork, forming a 4 cm-wide band. Machine topstitch close to edge and again 5 mm away on each long edge. This band forms top edge of apron bib.

Necktie
Cut a 110 x 10 cm strip in red fabric. With right sides together, pin one end along the side edge of patchwork block

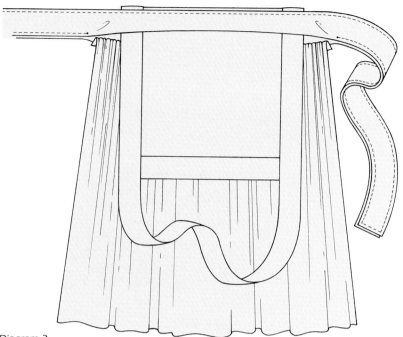

Diagram 2

for 26 cm to where it meets the finished top edge (Diagram 1). Repeat for other side of apron with the other end of the strip. Machine stitch; press and turn over, folding in half and turning under 1 cm seam allowance to form 4 cm band. Slip-stitch to machine stitching on either side of apron. Pin the remainder of the band together, turning in 1 cm seam allowances on either edge. Baste together and topstitch close to the edge and again 5 mm away on each edge along the entire length of band.

Skirt

Cut a 90 x 62 cm length of red fabric. Machine stitch a hem on each 62 cm edge for sides of apron skirt. Turn under 5 mm along a 90 cm edge for bottom hem, then a following 5 cm and machine stitch. Run two gathering threads along the top edge and pull up to 38 cm. To form apron ties, cut and join strips of fabric to give two 184 x 6 cm pieces.

With right sides together, pin centre of bib front to centre of one long pieced strip. Pin centre of remaining strip to wrong side of bib front and baste through the three thicknesses. Pin around

the tie bands, leaving an opening of 50 cm in the centre of the bottom edges of band. Machine stitch band.

Pin gathered skirt to the bottom front edge of band, right sides together, matching centres and adjusting gathers. Machine stitch (Diagram 2). Trim and press seam allowances away

from the skirt so that all raw edges will be held within the band. Trim band corners and seam allowances and turn through. Pin remainder of band and baste. Slip-stitch band into machine stitching along the apron skirt. Topstitch close to the edge and again 5 mm away along entire length of the band.

Diagram 1

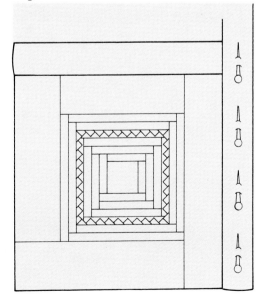

DRAWSTRING RIBBON POUCH

Little girls love drawstring bags to hang across their shoulders and keep all their treasures safe. Big girls love them too, especially for special evenings out. Scraps of pretty ribbons and a small amount of waterwave silk taffeta are all you need for this delicate pair.

Materials

For one bag.

Scraps of watermarked silk for bag and taffeta for lining; 40 cm lengths of assorted ribbons; 2.5 m of satin cord.

Method: Cut a 13 cm-diameter circle (see page 103) and a 40 x 27 cm rectangle from silk. Cut another set from lining fabric. Pin 40 cm lengths of ribbon across the width of the silk rectangle, leaving approx. 8 cm of silk uncovered at top edge. (See photograph.)

Instructions

For ribbon casement at top, cut two 17.5 cm lengths of approx. 2.5 cm-wide ribbon. Hem short ends. Pin one ribbon 2 cm in from raw edge of fabric along width of fabric and leaving a 1 cm gap. Pin 2nd ribbon along the same line (2 cm should be remaining on other raw edge of fabric). Stitch ribbons in place close to edges of ribbon.

Pin short sides of rectangle together with right sides facing and 1.5 cm seam allowance; stitch. Pin lower edge of rectangle to silk circle with right sides facing; stitch. Neaten seams and turn through to right side. Stitch lining together in the same way, leaving an opening in base for turning through.

Leave lining with wrong side out and place over bag so that right sides are facing. With 1 cm seams, stitch around top edge. Trim and pull bag through lining to right side. Slip-stitch opening closed. Cut cord in half and, following diagram, thread one length through whole ribbon casement; knot ends together. Thread second piece of cord through casement, beginning and ending in the opposite casement opening.

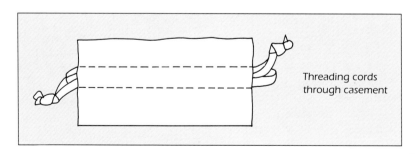

Threading cords through casement

Town and Country Bags

Soft fabric bags, one is big and roomy, the other is a classic style suitable for work or town. Both are made using a quick and easy method of machine patchwork and quilting combined, and each bag features a special closing frame.

COUNTRY BAG
FINISHED SIZE: approx. 40 cm high and 46 cm wide.
NOTE: 6 mm seam allowance included.

Materials

1 m each of three 115 cm-wide contrasting fabrics; 1 m of 115 cm-wide fourth contrast for lining; large snaplock*; 1 m of thin polyester wadding.

Instructions

From one contrasting fabric, cut two shoulder straps 80 x 11 cm. Cut two pieces of wadding the same size as the shoulder straps and tack to wrong side of straps. With right sides together, stitch one short edge and the long edge. Turn through so that seam sits in the middle of one side. Press lightly.

From each of the three fabrics, cut 115 cm-wide strips in widths of 2.5 cm, 3 cm, 4.5 cm and 5 cm. (Cut seven of each colour to start. You may need more later.) Place the wadding on the wrong side of the lining fabric and tack the two pieces together. Starting in the centre and working outwards, lay one strip diagonally on top of the wadding (see Diagram 1). Pin in place.

With right sides together and raw edges even, place the next strip (a different fabric) on top of the first strip. Stitch a 6 mm seam (this stitching will show through on the lining side). Turn the strip over to the right side. Press lightly on seamline. Attach the next strip in the same manner. Continue in alternating strips until one side of wadding is covered. Turn piece and repeat for other side of first diagonal strip. Cut fabric to fit pattern. Zigzag the long edges of the fabric, stitching all three layers together.

From same fabric as shoulder straps, cut two frill pieces 115 x 11 cm wide.

With right sides facing, stitch short ends. Turn through and, with raw edges even, stitch two gathering threads on the long raw edge, pull up gathers.

Lay pieced fabric flat with

strips facing you. Turning the zigzagged edge under, attach the frill to the long edge of the lining side of the fabric. Repeat for other frill on remaining long edge.

To form casing for snaplock frame, fold lining piece on long edge over 5 cm to strip-pieced fabric. Machine a row of stitching 2 cm from the folded top edge. Repeat for remaining long edge. Fold fabric in half, right sides together, and stitch to within 5 cm of top edge. Mitre corner by matching side seam to bottom fold (Diagram 2). Zigzag edges together. Attach shoulder straps at dots, placing the seam of the strap towards the lining. Slide the frame into the casing. Opposite ends of the frame fit just like a door hinge. Press ends of frame together to align holes. Slide the self-pivoting rivet through the holes.

* To purchase snaplock frames suitable for these bags contact Anne's Glory Box, 60 Beaumont St, Hamilton, Newcastle 2303. Ph. (049) 26 2203.

TOWN BAG
NOTE: 6 mm seam allowance included on pattern pieces.

Materials

30 cm of 115 cm-wide paisley

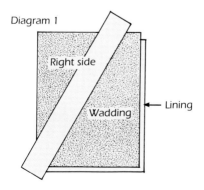

Diagram 1
Right side
Wadding
← Lining

Town and Country Bags (cont'd)

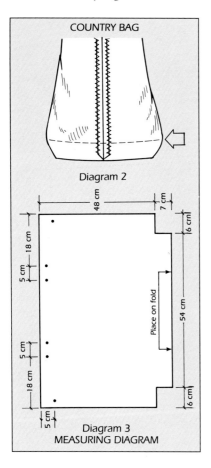

COUNTRY BAG

Diagram 2

Diagram 3
MEASURING DIAGRAM

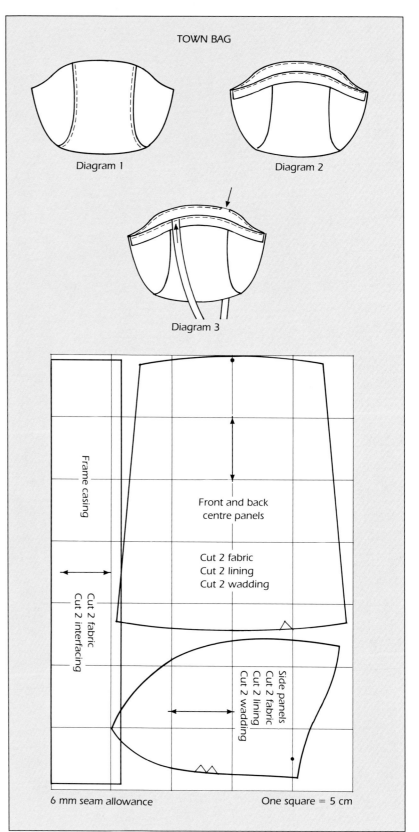

TOWN BAG

Diagram 1

Diagram 2

Diagram 3

Frame casing

Cut 2 fabric
Cut 2 interfacing

Front and back
centre panels

Cut 2 fabric
Cut 2 lining
Cut 2 wadding

Side panels
Cut 2 fabric
Cut 2 lining
Cut 2 wadding

6 mm seam allowance

One square = 5 cm

fabric; 30 cm of 115 cm-wide co-ordinating fabric; 30 cm of 115 cm-wide fabric for bag lining; 50 cm each of thin wadding and fusible interfacing; small snaplock frame.

Instructions

Enlarge and cut pattern pieces from fabrics, wadding and interfacing as required, transferring all markings. Cut lining, wadding and interfacing pieces 6 mm smaller than outer fabric pieces. For bag strap, cut one piece 90 x 6 cm. Place interfacing between wrong sides of centre and side panels and wadding. Fuse layers together by steam pressing, using a damp pressing cloth. Using diagonal

Country Bag, left and Town Bag, right.

rows of stitching 2 cm apart, quilt side panels (not lining pieces). With right sides together and matching notches, stitch centre panels together. With right sides together, stitch two side panels together at notched seam. Repeat for remaining side panels. With right sides together, stitch side pieces to centre piece (Diagram 1). Fuse interfacing to wrong side of lining front and back panels. With right sides together, stitch these two panels together from the raw edges, leaving the centre section open. Fuse interfacing to wrong side of frame casing, folding short edges 1 cm to wrong side of fabric. With wrong sides together and raw edges even, fold in half lengthwise. Centring frame casing and having raw edges even, stitch frame casing to outer bag (Diagram 2).

Fold strap in half lengthways so that the raw edges meet in the centre. Fold in half again and stitch close to the folded edge. Double-stitch each end of strap to opposite sides of centre panels at dots (Diagram 3). With right sides together (placing one inside the other), stitch upper edge of bag to upper edge of lining. Turn right side out through opening in lining. Slip-stitch opening together. Slide frame through casing, matching the opposite ends of the frame. Press opposite ends of the frame together to align holes. Slide the self-pivoting rivets through the holes to secure the frame.

Gifts to Make

Gifts you make yourself are always appreciated, and they usually last longer than their store-bought equivalent because of the quality of the materials and their hand finishing. Patchwork gifts are often very inexpensive to make as many of them can be put together from scraps or small pieces of fabric.

CRAZY PATCHWORK DECORATIONS

Handmade Christmas decorations and cards will be treasured and brought out for display every season for many years to come. Use leftover scraps of Christmas fabric to create a crazy patchwork piece, which can then be cut up into a variety of shapes for tree decorations, a wreath or handmade greeting cards.

Materials
Cotton calico (pre-shrunk) base fabric piece—the size of this piece determines the finished size of your crazy patchwork piece; scraps of Christmas print fabrics; sequins, stars and beads; gold and silver thread; polyester fibrefill.
Wreath: 1 m each of 5 mm-wide red and green satin ribbon; 1 m of 6 cm-wide red satin ribbon; bought twig wreath.
Cards: Medium-weight cardboard 23 x 16 cm, or desired size.

Instructions
To make crazy patchwork
The base fabric will be the finished size of your crazy patchwork piece. Cut Christmas print fabric into random shapes and attach to base fabric, using a straight machine stitch. Stitch sequins, stars and beads at random on fabric. Embroider overlapping fabric edges with rows of embroidery stitch. We used feather-stitch, blanket-stitch and herringbone-stitch in gold and silver thread. Alternatively, you could use decorative machine stitches.

Decorations
Cut a front and back motif from crazy patchwork fabric. Placing motifs wrong sides together, fill with small amount of fibrefill. Using zigzag-stitch, machine motifs together close to edge. Trim raw edges. With gold thread, make a hanging loop at the top.

Wreath
Wind narrow red and green satin ribbon around wreath: glue ends to back of wreath.
Make motifs as for decorations, omitting hanging loop. Glue to wreath in positions desired. Finish with a big red bow. Glue stars and sequins at random to wreath.

Cards
Cut medium-weight cardboard 23 x 16 cm or desired size for card. Cut one of each motif from crazy patchwork fabric. Position on cardboard, placing small amount of fibrefill under motif. Using zigzag-stitch, machine through cardboard close to motif edge.

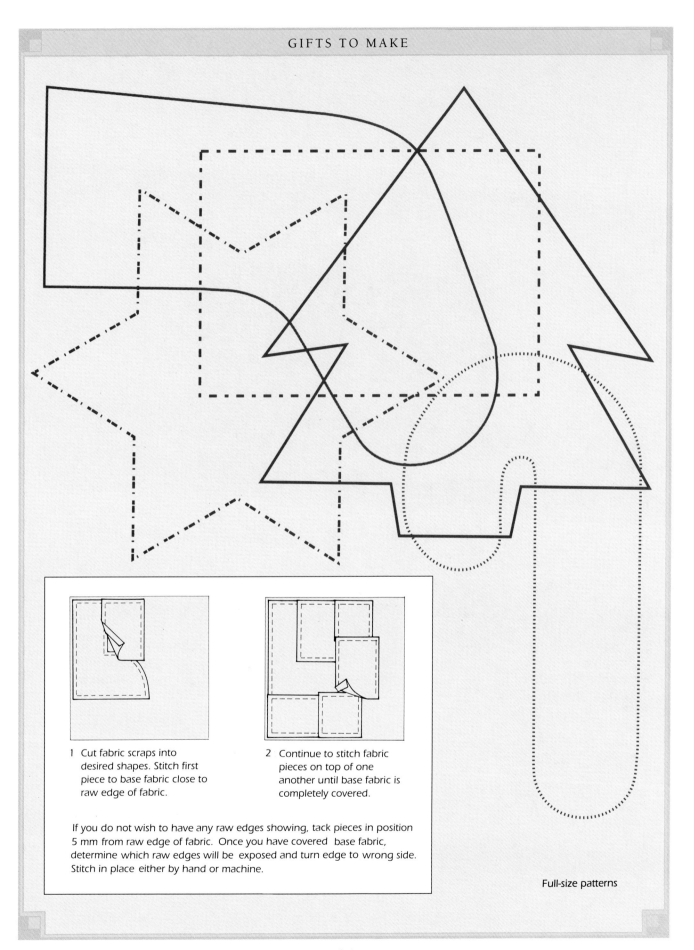

1 Cut fabric scraps into desired shapes. Stitch first piece to base fabric close to raw edge of fabric.

2 Continue to stitch fabric pieces on top of one another until base fabric is completely covered.

If you do not wish to have any raw edges showing, tack pieces in position 5 mm from raw edge of fabric. Once you have covered base fabric, determine which raw edges will be exposed and turn edge to wrong side. Stitch in place either by hand or machine.

Full-size patterns

ℙATCHWORK 𝔸DVENT 𝕋REE

𝔗his delightful fabric Christmas tree has twenty-five hearts whose pockets you can fill with small trinkets or lollies for the children to remove each day of December. When they are all gone Christmas will be here. The matching tree decorations are made from the same heart pattern.

FINISHED SIZE: approx. 70 x 55 cm.

Materials

1.5 m of 90 cm-wide calico; 80 x 60 cm piece of polyester wadding; 30 cm of 90 cm-wide green plaid fabric; 10 cm each of three 90 cm-wide red plaid fabrics; 2.3 m of piping cord; 2 cm-diameter plastic ring; 14 small bells; 2.5 m of 5 mm-wide red satin ribbon; water-soluble craft pen.

Instructions

Trace heart shape onto paper using the heart diagram. Cut 11 green plaid fabric hearts, adding 6 mm seam allowance. Cut 14 assorted red plaid fabric hearts from the three fabrics, adding seam allowance. Cut 26 corresponding calico hearts for backing. With right sides facing, stitch calico backing to each heart, leaving a small opening on the side. Clip curves and trim points; turn hearts through. Slip-stitch opening closed and press.

Make tree pattern from the diagram, adding 5 cm seam allowance all around. Draw a grid of 7.5 cm squares on the tree (as indicated on diagram). Cut calico using this pattern and mark out squares on fabric using a water-soluble craft pen.

Cut a second piece of calico the same size for the backing. Cut wadding to fit tree and baste to the wrong side of tree front. Machine topstitch through both layers along all of the grid lines to quilt the fabric. Handstitch one heart to the centre of each 7.5 cm square, leaving the top of the heart open to form a pocket. Cut 4 cm strips of green plaid fabric and join to make a 2.3 m piece. Lay piping cord on the wrong side of fabric strip; pin wrong sides together and using a zipper foot, machine-stitch close to piping cord (see page 102).

Machine-stitch piping around front edge of tree (raw edges towards the outer edge). Overlap ends where they meet. With right sides facing and with piping facing inward, machine-stitch tree front to tree

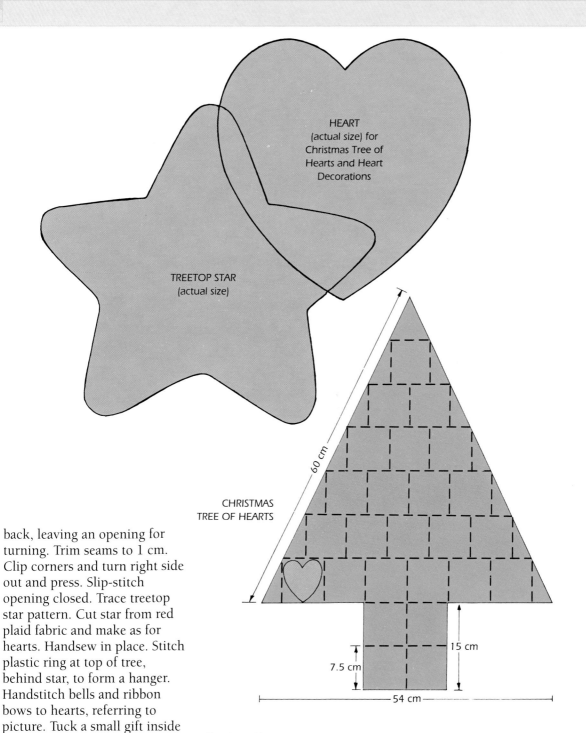

HEART
(actual size) for
Christmas Tree of
Hearts and Heart
Decorations

TREETOP STAR
(actual size)

*CHRISTMAS
TREE OF HEARTS*

60 cm

15 cm

7.5 cm

54 cm

back, leaving an opening for turning. Trim seams to 1 cm. Clip corners and turn right side out and press. Slip-stitch opening closed. Trace treetop star pattern. Cut star from red plaid fabric and make as for hearts. Handsew in place. Stitch plastic ring at top of tree, behind star, to form a hanger. Handstitch bells and ribbon bows to hearts, referring to picture. Tuck a small gift inside each heart pocket.

HEART DECORATIONS

Materials

Red and green fabric scraps; polyester fibre filling; narrow ribbon or cord.

Instructions

Using actual-size pattern, cut hearts from fabric scraps, adding 1 cm seam allowance. Place two hearts right sides together and stitch around, leaving a small opening. Turn through to right side and trim

seams. Stuff with fibre filling and stitch opening closed. Thread a tapestry needle with a length of ribbon or cord. Slip this through the centre top of the heart. Knot ends of the ribbon to form a loop for hanging.

PATCHWORK PUSS

Patchwork Puss with her extra long tail has been made from mauve-coloured scraps of pretty Liberty fabrics. Use the triangle shape provided and if you would like to make a larger pussycat, simply double all measurements and materials.

FINISHED SIZE: approx. 20 cm high.

Materials

10 cm each of four 115 cm-wide printed lawn fabrics; polyester fibre filling; ribbon.

Instructions

Trace triangle pattern and cut out in cardboard. Cut out 20 triangles of each fabric, positioning the pattern arrow on the straight grain of the fabric.

Machine-stitch triangles together to make 40 squares using 6 mm seam allowance. Join 20 squares to make a rectangle of five rows of four

squares. Repeat with the remaining squares.

Enlarge cat pattern (see below) and cut out in paper, adding 6 mm seam allowance. Cut out two cat shapes from the patchwork, reversing the pattern to get a front and back. Machine the cats together, leaving a 7 cm opening at the base. Clip curves, turn to right side and fill. Slip-stitch opening closed and add a ribbon tie.

Full-size pattern

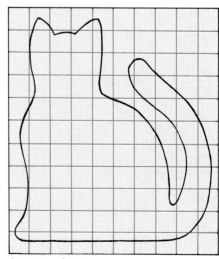

1 square = 2 cm

CRAZY PATCHWORK BOX LID

Vividly coloured silks embellished with hand embroidery and trinkets decorate the lid of this handcrafted oak box. Luxurious silk ribbons and threads, tiny buttons and glass bugle beads all combine with a variety of embroidery stitches for a very rich and highly decorative look. You could use the same technique to make evening bags, belts, cushion covers and if you're really ambitious even a quilt.

NOTE: 6 mm seam allowance used. Fabric showing on lid measures 24 x 14 cm.

Materials

Scraps of fabrics (we used silks and satins to give a rich, jewelled appearance), ribbons, beads, embroidery, threads, laces, buttons, almost anything you would like to stitch onto your fabric; calico scrap (to fit our box lid 26 x 16 cm); polyester wadding; fabric glue; fine timber tacks.

Instructions

Cut a centre piece in dark fabric (any size) with at least five angles. Pin to calico, wrong sides facing. Cut the first shape and lay it against the first angle, right sides together. Stitch. Turn to right side, press. Working in a clockwise direction, cut shapes and stitch in place, making sure that the new shape extends beyond the previous shape(s). Trim any excess fabric from previous shapes as you go.

This will make the piece easier to embroider. Continue in this manner until calico is completely covered. Trim excess fabric to shape of calico. Zigzag or overlock edges if desired. Embroider and stitch ribbons, laces, buttons, beads, etc., on patchworked piece. Cut three or four pieces of wadding to same size as calico.

Dab fabric glue around inside edge of box lid. Place patchworked piece right side down into lid and press edges to glue. Allow to dry. Place wadding pieces in position; place timber backing piece on top of wadding and tack in position.

Folded Star Patchwork Key Ring and Purse

This pretty matching accessory set is a lovely gift to give or receive. Made from a folded patchwork technique, you use very small amounts of four different fabrics for the patched effect. Small velcro dots are used to keep the coin purse closed.

PURSE

Materials

Scraps of four different patchwork fabrics; 10 x 3 cm piece of velcro; cardboard.

Instructions

Make a 5 cm square template and a 9 x 5 cm rectangular template from cardboard. Referring to picture and diagram for colours, cut four squares from fabric 1, six squares from fabrics 2 and 3 and four rectangles from fabric 4. Fold pieces as follows.

Square

Place square of fabric face down on ironing board; bring top edge down to bottom edge to fold square in half horizontally; press; fold again in half vertically; press and pin.

Triangle

Press fabric square in half horizontally; bring top corners of fabric down to meet at the centre of bottom edges; press and pin.

Strip

Press fabric rectangle in half lengthwise, wrong sides together, pin.

Fabric 1

Fabric 2

Fabric 3

Fabric 4

Fold pieces as described to form four squares from fabric 1 pieces, four squares and two triangles each from fabrics 2 and 3 and four strips from fabric 4. Cut a 9 cm square of fabric for block backing. Using a craft pen, mark horizontal and vertical centre lines on right side of backing.

To assemble block for purse
Referring to diagram and working from the centre outwards, pin two squares in fabric 1 and two squares in fabric 2 to backing so that folded corners meet at the centre. Tack centres and outer corners to backing, being careful not to let tacking show (as it remains in fabric).

Pin remaining squares in fabrics 1 and 2 in place, *overlapping* centre squares, so that inner corners are 5 mm

from centre of design and outer edges extend 5 mm beyond first squares. Tack down corners as before. Pin two strips each in fabric 4 to top and bottom of design, overlapping second squares 1 cm and first squares 5 mm with folded edges; raw edges should be even with the backing block. Tack in place. Attach strips in fabric 4 to each side in the same way. Pin and tack fabric 3 squares to corners of design matching outer edges. Pin triangles in fabric 3 in place on top and bottom of design and fabric 2 triangles to sides of design, keeping all outer edges even; tack in place. Topstitch 5 mm from block edges all around.

To make up purse
Cut four 13 cm squares for purse front, back and two lining pieces. For patchwork 'frame', cut away a centre square from front piece 1 cm smaller all round than patchwork. Clipping as necessary, fold 6 mm seam allowance to wrong side of fabric and press. Topstitch frame to completed patchwork close to inner edge. Pin lining fabric pieces to purse back and front with wrong sides together.

Press top edges 1 cm towards lining side; pin. Pin velcro strip—half to each side—inside top edge. Topstitch close to long edges through all thicknesses. With right sides together, pin

purse front and back together and stitch 5 mm side and bottom seams. Finish edges with a zigzag stitch.

KEY RING

Materials
Fabric scraps in four different patchwork fabrics; 10 cm of 6 mm-wide ribbon; large slip-ring for keys.

Instructions
Referring to directions given for purse, make a miniature block using 2.5 cm-square and 5 x 3 cm templates; make 5 cm-square backing. Cut 5 cm-square piece of fabric for key ring back. From the same fabric, cut 2.5 cm-wide bias strips to fit around block, plus 1 cm.

With wrong sides together, pin backing to made-up block; tack close to raw edges. Cut ribbon in half to make two 5 cm lengths. Pin and baste on top of each other to one end of block at centre (top) with raw edges even; leave other end free.

Press one long and one short edge of bias strip 5 mm to wrong side. Beginning at centre top with raw end, pin the bias strip around block, right sides together and raw edges even, overlapping ends. Stitch strip in place 5 mm from edge, leaving ribbon ends free.

Turn strip over, mitring corners, and slip-stitch in place. Place slip-ring onto ribbon and tuck free ribbon ends under fold before stitching centre top.

POTPOURRI-FILLED SACHETS

Who can ever tire of sweetly scented potpourri sachets? Hung in your wardrobe, or placed in a drawer they give a subtle scent to everything around them. Spoil your female friends and family members by using soft satin silk and fine cotton lace to make these very pretty cathedral window pattern sachets.

Materials

30 cm of 115 cm-wide silk fabric; scrap of 2.5 cm-wide lace; 20 cm of 1 cm-wide ribbon; potpourri.

Instructions

Cut two 22 cm squares in fabric. Fold one in half, right sides facing, and stitch short ends by hand or machine using a 3 mm seam (Diagram 1). Press the seams open and fold the fabric so the remaining sides can be stitched together, leaving an opening to turn through (Diagram 2). Trim seams on corners and turn through. Fold corners of square to the centre (Diagram 3). Stitch the four points together at the centre with a decorative stitch to secure (Diagram 4). Repeat with second square of fabric.

Place the two squares right sides together and oversew one edge securely from corner to corner (Diagram 5).

Cut 10 cm square in lace or desired fabric and place square over the seam between the two folded fabric squares (Diagram 6). Pin in place and curl pack one edge of the folded square onto the lace and stitch in place through all thicknesses. With right side of completed window facing you, fold short ends to meet at centre (piece will now form a square).

Hand-oversew top and bottom edges. Turn through to right side.

Fill centre with potpourri and oversew remaining seam closed. With 10 cm square of lace, repeat steps to form 'window'. Attach ribbon hanger.

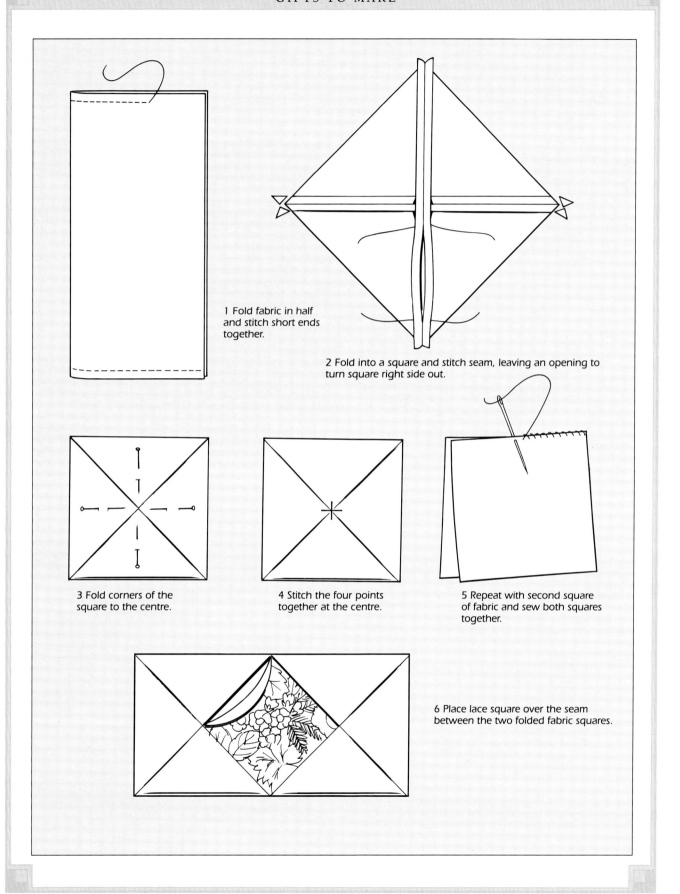

1 Fold fabric in half and stitch short ends together.

2 Fold into a square and stitch seam, leaving an opening to turn square right side out.

3 Fold corners of the square to the centre.

4 Stitch the four points together at the centre.

5 Repeat with second square of fabric and sew both squares together.

6 Place lace square over the seam between the two folded fabric squares.

Nine Patch Doll's Quilt

This miniature quilt makes a very special present for your favourite little girl, or you could even make it as a wallhanging. Quick and easy to construct, you can then concentrate on practising your quilting stitch.

FINISHED SIZE: 94 cm square.
NOTE: 6 mm seam allowance used. This needs to be added to all pattern pieces.

Materials

2 m of 115 cm-wide white cotton fabric; 1 m of 115 cm-wide blue print cotton fabric; 100 cm square of wadding; 4 m of 6 cm-wide bias cut fabric or bias binding.

Instructions

Make templates for three shapes, 16 cm and 4 cm squares, and a 16 x 4 cm rectangle. Cut one 16 cm square from print fabric, twenty 4 cm squares from print fabric, and sixteen 4 cm squares from white fabric, eight rectangles in white and four rectangles from print fabric. Piece together to form three rows, then stitch rows together to make centre block. Cut four 40 x 10 cm white strips and two 40 x 6 cm print strips. Stitch one print strip between two white strips. Repeat with remaining strips. Stitch to two opposite sides of centre block. Cut four 92 x 10 cm white strips and two 92 x 10 cm print strips. Attach as before to remaining sides of centre block. If you are going to quilt the finished piece place quilting pattern on patched piece now, before assembly. Cut wadding and white backing fabric to same size as finished patched piece. Sandwich wadding between layers and pin then tack in a sunburst pattern (see page 101). Quilt as desired. With wrong sides together, fold bias in half. Using a 1 cm-wide seam stitch to quilt edge having all raw edges even and right sides together. Turn folded edge of bias to back of quilt and stitch in place.

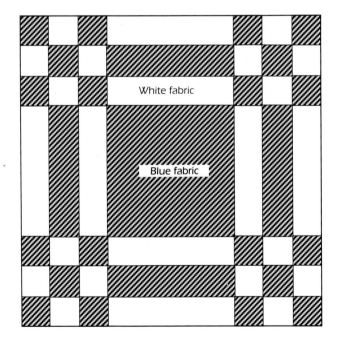

White fabric

Blue fabric

PATCHWORK SOFT TOYS

You can use pieces of old worn quilts or make a new quilted patchwork piece to create these old fashioned soft toys. Give them a real country look by using simple ginghams and checks, or if you don't want to go to that much trouble you can use one of the many printed patchwork lookalike fabrics available.

NOTE: These pieces were made
from a worn quilt. However,
you could make your own
patchwork pieces or buy printed
fabric which simulates patched
fabric and quilt it.
FINISHED SIZE: duck approx.
45 cm long, 30 cm high; cow
approx. 47 cm long, 33 cm high.

Materials

Duck: 70 x 55 cm piece quilted
patchwork fabric; filling; small
amount of embroidery thread
for eye. Cow: 1 m x 70 cm piece
quilted patchwork fabric; filling;
ball of yarn for plaited tail.

Instructions

DUCK

Enlarge and transfer patterns,
adding 6 mm seam allowance to
all pieces. Embroider eye using
satin-stitch. Cut out pieces and
zigzag or overlock all raw edges
to prevent fraying. With right
sides facing, stitch two duck
wings together, leaving a small
gap for turning. Trim seams, turn
through. Repeat for bill, tail and
foot. With right sides together,
pin gusset to underside of one
duck shape, placing the
squared-off end of the gusset at
the tip of the duck's tail. Ease to
fit and stitch. Repeat for other
side of gusset and then stitch
remaining open edges together
leaving an opening for filling.
Fill duck, slip-stitch opening
closed. Slip-stitch bill, tail and
foot in place at marked points.

COW

With right sides together, stitch
cow shapes, leaving an opening
for filling. Turn right side out,
fill cow, slip-stitch opening
closed. Plait yarn for tail in
desired thickness and length.
Slip-stitch ear and tail in place.

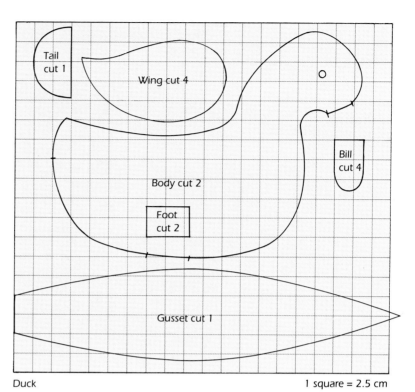

Duck   1 square = 2.5 cm

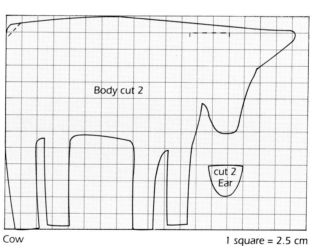

Cow   1 square = 2.5 cm

General Instructions

We often refer to patchwork and quilting in the same breath, but in fact they are two very different techniques. A piece of work, if patched, does not have to be quilted, while quilting is not worked exclusively on patched fabric. A simple definition of each is that patchwork is the method of joining smaller pieces of fabric to form a large piece, while quilting is the decorative process of securing layers together. Traditionally quilting is done by hand with small running-stitches; however, it can also be successfully done on a sewing machine.

PATCHWORK

Materials

Needles
For hand-sewing, short fine needles known as 'betweens' are best as they slip in and out of the fabric easily. Size 8 is recommended for beginners while experienced quilters who want to make smaller stitches usually use a size 10. If machining, use a needle size compatible with the fabric thickness.

Thimble
If you are hand-sewing it is advisable to protect your fingers with a thimble. It should fit comfortably on your middle finger. Some quilters also like to use a thimble on the index finger on the hand which works below the quilt.

Pins
Glass headed pins are ideal as they are easily seen and removed from the work and they slide through the layers easily. Never use rusted pins or leave pins and needles in your work for long periods of time as they are likely to rust and permanently stain the fabric.

Quarter Seamer
This is a short perspex rod which is a quarter of an inch (6 mm) wide on all four sides. It enables you to rule seam allowances quickly and accurately.

Clear plastic ruler
Make sure it is well marked, ideally with both metric and imperial measurements, as they are still both commonly used in patchwork.

Thread
If you are hand-sewing use a quilting thread for all seams. It is stronger than normal thread and less likely to curl up, knot and break. You can also run your normal machine thread through beeswax (available at craft shops) to strengthen it and prevent it from knotting. When using a variety of different coloured fabrics stitch your seams using a thread matching the darkest-coloured fabric.

Fabrics
Originally patchwork pieces were mostly made from scraps, but today most projects use new fabrics. The best fabrics to use are medium-weight 100 per cent cotton. These wear better, last longer and are the easiest to handle. Many craft shops and fabric shops stock fabrics specifically designed for patchwork in a myriad of colours and designs. Always purchase the best quality fabric you can afford.

For ideas on colour and design look at patchwork books, exhibitions and shops to get ideas on how colour and pattern work. You could draw and colour a design or make a miniature of your design by cutting small pieces of fabric and glueing them to paper.

If you are new to patchwork, start with a small project you can complete without too much difficulty. As your skills and experience develop and your confidence builds, you will be able to embark on more difficult projects and experiment with different fabrics. Beautiful effects can be achieved with other fabric types, such as satins and velvets, however their use is recommended only for experienced sewers.

Pre-shrink all fabrics and test them for colour-fastness. It is better to find out that a fabric is unsuitable before you begin a project than after you have put many hours of work into it.

Templates
Templates are patterns of the pieces you are going to stitch together. They are usually made of cardboard, sandpaper or plastic, or you can purchase certain shapes made of thin metal. Craft shops sell plastic suitable for making patchwork and quilting templates.

Those used for hand-sewing, appliqué and quilting are cut to the exact shape, and do not include a seam allowance. Use a lead or special marking pencil to trace around your template. The outline of the shape is used as a guide for stitching, to ensure accuracy. The 6 mm seam allowance is marked easily around the template with a quarter seamer. Templates made for machine sewing include a 6 mm seam allowance—the guide on the machine will enable you to sew your pieces together accurately.

Make sure you keep your original pattern intact when making templates, so that you can check your templates for accuracy against it. Transfer all markings, including grainline, letter number, pattern name and number of pieces that need to be cut, onto each template. If you need to cut a piece in the reverse, or need a mirror image, put the letter R on the template with the number of the pieces required.

Cutting
Use a fine sharp pencil to mark

your fabrics on the wrong side. A lead or pale coloured pencil works well, with silver or white showing easily on dark fabrics. When cutting fabric use sharp scissors or a rotary cutter and board. Keep a pair of paper scissors for cutting templates and a small, sharp, pointed pair of embroidery scissors for trimming threads and clipping points and seam allowances.

The most economical cutting plan is to cut out borders and sashings (or tracks) before you cut the small pieces. Cut squares and rectangles on the straight grain. Right angle triangles should have the right angle on the straight grain, while other triangles and irregular shapes should have the straight grain of the fabric running through their centres.

When cutting small pieces of fabric using templates make a sandpaper covered board. Cover a piece of plywood or craftwood with glued pieces of sandpaper. Place fabric wrong side up when tracing around templates. The sandpaper will 'grab' the fabric and prevent it from slipping, keeping your markings much more accurate.

Assembly
When hand-sewing seams use a small even running-stitch, secured every few stitches by a back-stitch. When machining use an average-sized stitch compatible with the fabrics you are working with. To make seams strong, do not press them open. Press them to one side, preferably toward the darker piece of fabric so that they will not show through. Wherever possible join fabric in units to form strips. Don't try to fit a

square into an angled corner made of three squares which have been joined. Join squares in straight rows within each block, then join blocks into strips. At cross seams, alternate the direction of the seam allowance to distribute the bulk of the fabric more evenly. You may even need to trim the seam allowance, particularly if a number of seams are coming into a point. Press each seam as it is completed.

QUILTING

Items can be quilted by hand or machine. When quilting by hand a small even running-stitch is used.

Materials

Thread
As for patchwork. Quilters' thread is available in a wide variety of colours.

Needles
As for patchwork.

Hoop
To keep your work flat you need to work on some type of frame, either a hoop or a floor frame. Hoops are ideal as they are easily transportable and can be moved around the work as desired. Floor frames are great if you are tackling a large project such as a quilt, however you need to have the room to keep them set up on a fairly permanent basis while you are quilting.

Wadding
Polyester batting or wadding is most commonly used. It comes in a variety of

thicknesses and sizes. You can now purchase pieces specifically cut for different quilt sizes so that you don't have to join it yourself. To join pieces of wadding, butt edges and herringbone-stitch together. The backing fabric used should be compatible with the top layer. Pre-wash and join if necessary.

Preparation for quilting
Thorough preparation for quilting ensures a good result. Always prepare your quilting in the following manner, regardless of the size:
• Lay backing piece flat, right side down. Place wadding on top. Place fabric to be quilted on top, wrong side to wadding. Smooth out the fullness from centre to sides.
• Starting at the centre, pin then tack the layers together in a sunburst pattern (see diagram).
• Always begin quilting in the centre of the work.

Sunburst pattern

Hand quilting
A sign of good quilting is fine regular stitches and invisible thread joins. Each thread should start and finish with a small knot buried deep in the layers.

Machine quilting

Take the time to secure the layers thoroughly, working extra rows of basting 10 cm apart horizontally and diagonally. This prevents fabric slippage which is one of the most common problems with machine quilting. A space bar on your machine will simplify straight-line quilting. You'll need lots of tabletop space around your machine to support your work as you sew.

Roll work tightly from the edge to the centre, and place the roll under the arm of the machine. Work from the centre to the edge unrolling as you go. When you have finished quilting remove all basting and wash work if necessary to remove quilting lines.

To make piping

The thickness of your piping is determined by the thickness of your cord. Fold a corner of fabric over cord and pin close to the cord (Diagram 1). Measure 6 mm from pin and cut fabric. Open out this piece of fabric and use to determine the width of bias (Diagram 2).

TO MAKE PIPING AND BIAS

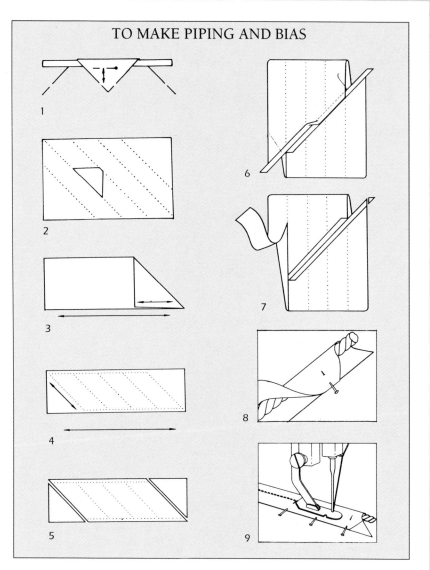

PATCHWORK AND QUILTING GROUPS

If you are keen to get more information on patchwork and quilting than this book offers, or wish to join a group or visit exhibitions of patchwork and quilting anywhere in Australia, write to The Quilters' Guild Inc, PO Box 654 Neutral Bay Junction NSW 2089.

Bias strips

These are bands cut on the cross-grain of the fabric. They give a degree of stretch to woven fabrics and are often used in areas where there are curves.

This is a useful technique for making large amounts of bias. To find the true bias of the fabric, fold fabric diagonally so that a straight edge on the fabric width is parallel to the selvedge (Diagram 3).

Press fabric along the diagonal fold. Open it out and mark parallel lines the desired width, using the crease as a guide (Diagram 4).

Mark 6 mm seam allowance on the lengthwise grain along each edge. Trim excess fabric diagonally at fold line (Diagram 5).

With right sides facing, fold fabric into a tube, aligning seams and marks but having one strip width extending beyond the edge on each side. Stitch and press seam open (Diagram 6).

Beginning at one end, cut along marked line until you reach the end of the strip (Diagram 7).

With wrong sides of fabric facing and raw edges even, pin cord inside bias strip (Diagram 8).

Using a zipper foot, stitch close to the cord (Diagram 9).

STITCH GUIDE

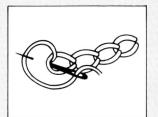

Chain-stitch

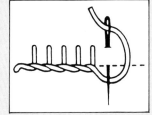

Blanket-stitch

Couching

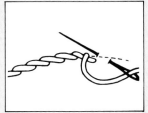

Stem-stitch

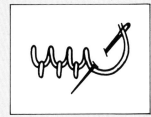

Parallel feather-stitch

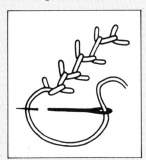

Feather-stitch

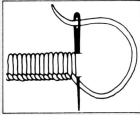

Buttonhole-stitch

Herringbone-stitch

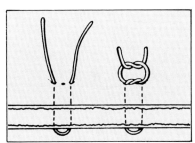

Tying a quilt with one thread

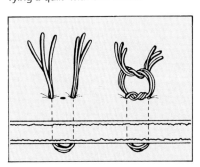

Tying a quilt with more than one thread

QUILT EDGES

We recommend finishing the edges with bias binding. Use either a commercial bias binding or a self-fabric binding.

To apply bias:

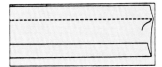

1. Lay bias on wrong side of quilt edge with raw edges even. Stitch.

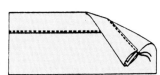

2. Turn bias strip to right side, turn under a seam allowance and stitch close to the edge.

HOW TO CUT A CIRCLE

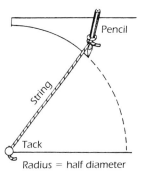

Pencil
String
Tack
Radius = half diameter

TRANSFERRING DESIGNS

Tape your design to a window with the wrong side against the glass. Positioning the fabric carefully, tape it over the design, right side facing you, and trace the design with either a soft lead pencil or a water-soluble craft pen. Check the solubility of your pen in an inconspicuous area of your fabric before you begin.

ENLARGING DESIGNS

To enlarge patterns with grids— small squares laid over the design—draw a grid of your own on tissue or brown paper, following the scale indicated on the pattern. For example, if the scale is '1 square = 2.5 cm', draw a series of 2.5 cm squares on your pattern paper to enlarge the drawing to the rec- ommended size.

First count the number of horizontal and vertical rows of squares on the original pattern. With a rule, mark the exact same number of horizontal and vertical rows of larger squares on the pattern paper.

Number horizontal and ver- tical rows of squares in the margin of the original pat- tern. Then transfer these numbers to corresponding rows on your pattern.

Alternatively, you can by in- expensive graph paper or boards from art supply shops and sta- tionery suppliers. They are available in 1 mm, 5 mm, 1 cm and 5 cm size grids.

To copy design onto your grid, begin by finding a square on your grid which corresponds with a square on the original. Mark your grid wherever a design line intersects a line on the original. It helps to visually divide every line into quarters to gauge whether the design line cuts the grid line halfway or somewhere in between.

Working one square at a time, mark each grid line where it is intersected by the design. After marking several squares, connect the dots, following the contours of the original. Work in pencil so you can erase mistakes.

Patterns without grids can be

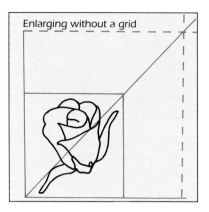

Enlarging without a grid

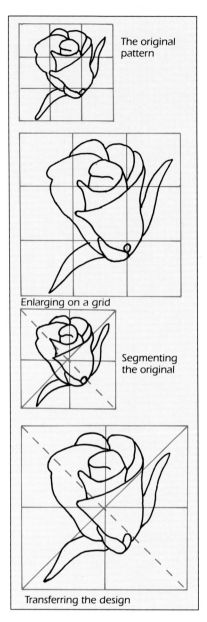

The original pattern

Enlarging on a grid

Segmenting the original

Transferring the design

enlarged if you know any one of the dimensions of the final pat- tern. First draw a box around the design. Then draw a di- agonal line between two corners. On the pattern paper, draw a right angle and extend the bottom line to the width you want the new design to be. Draw a vertical line from this point, making it roughly the same length as your extended bottom line. Lay the original in

the corner and, using a rule, extend the diagonal until it dis- sects the vertical. Extend left side of right angle to a point op- posite where the diagonal line meets the vertical line, then rule a horizontal line between these two points.

Divide the original pattern and the new pattern into quar- ters, number the sections, and transfer the design as explained above.

TEMPLATES

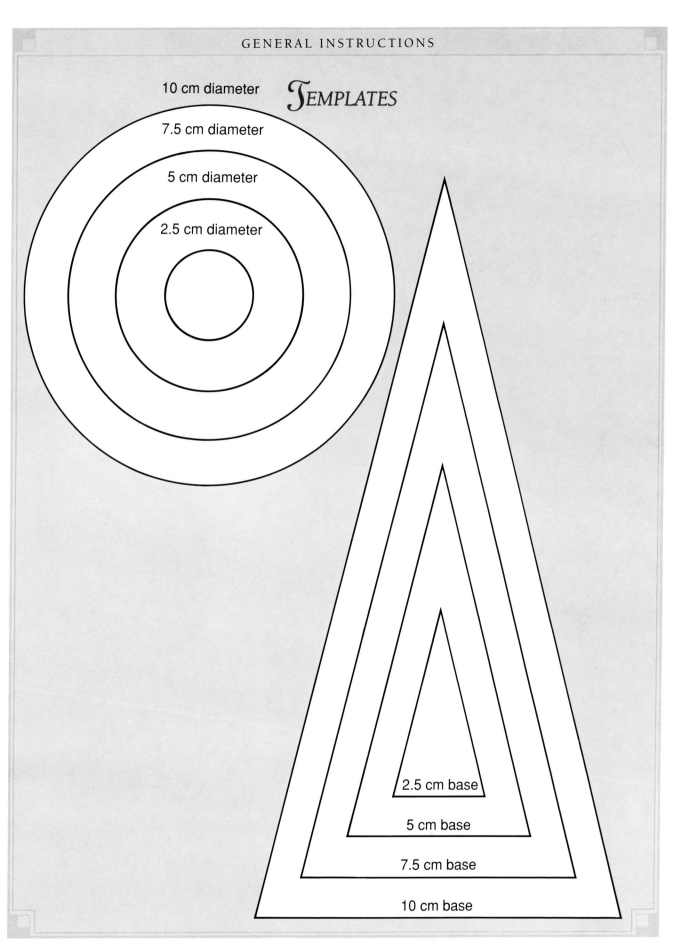

10 cm diameter

7.5 cm diameter

5 cm diameter

2.5 cm diameter

2.5 cm base

5 cm base

7.5 cm base

10 cm base

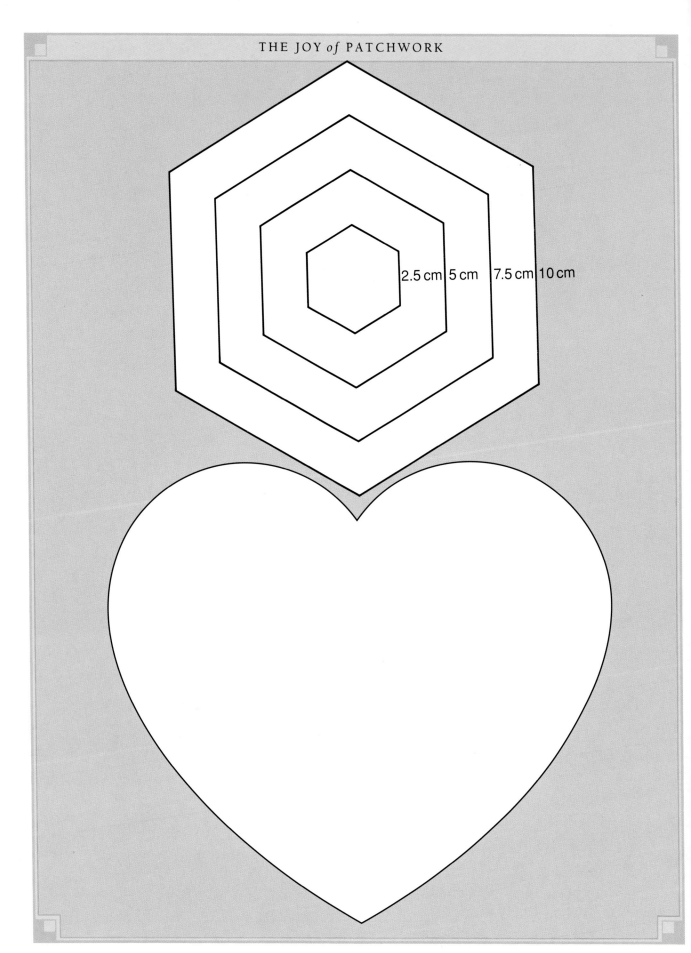

2.5 cm   5 cm   7.5 cm   10 cm

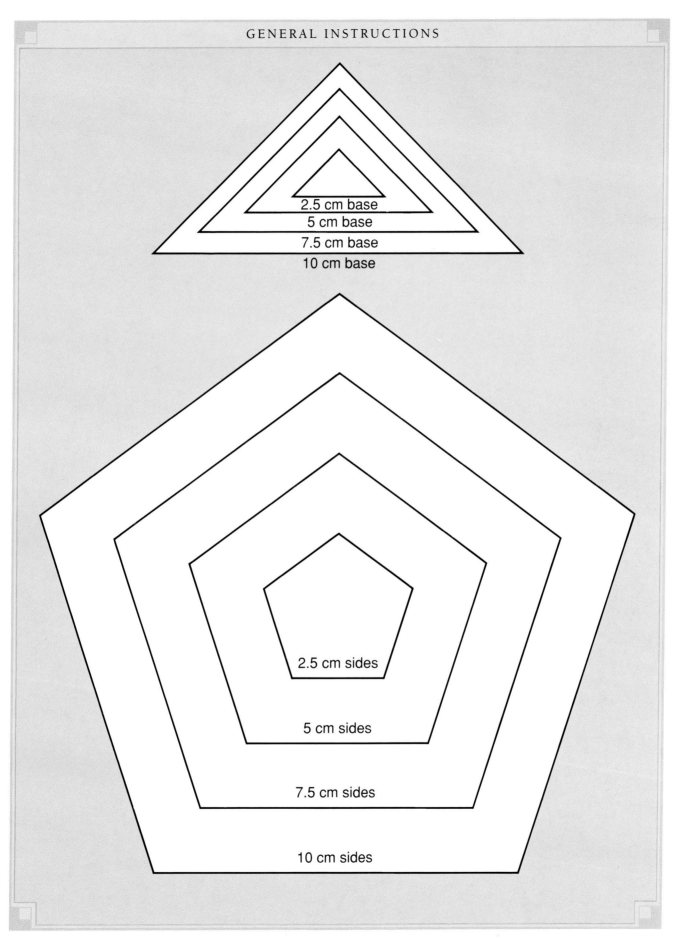

2.5 cm base
5 cm base
7.5 cm base
10 cm base

2.5 cm sides

5 cm sides

7.5 cm sides

10 cm sides

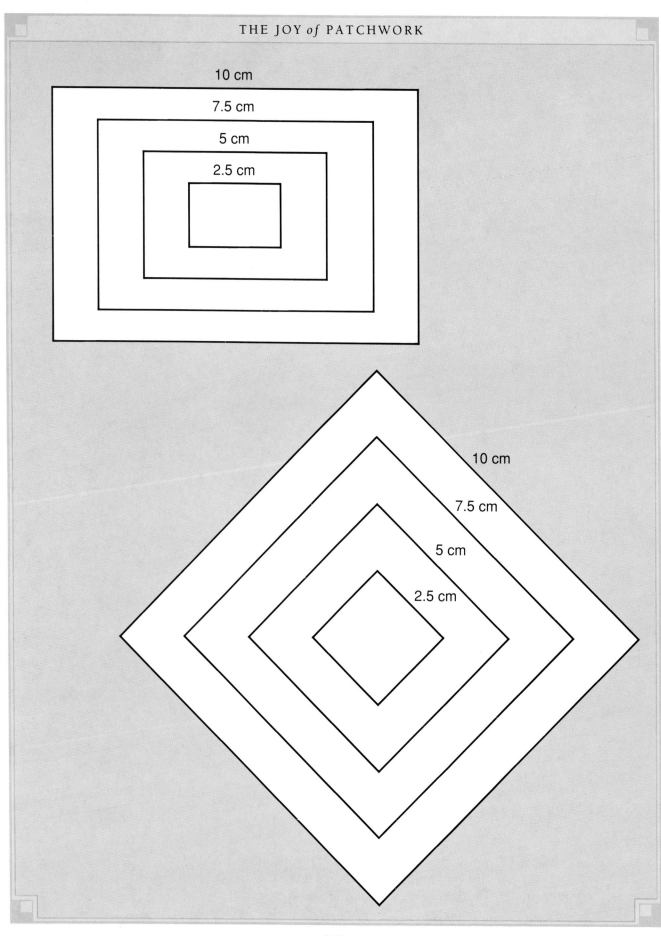

10 cm

7.5 cm

5 cm

2.5 cm

10 cm

7.5 cm

5 cm

2.5 cm

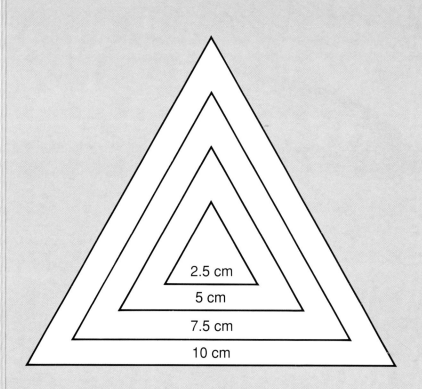

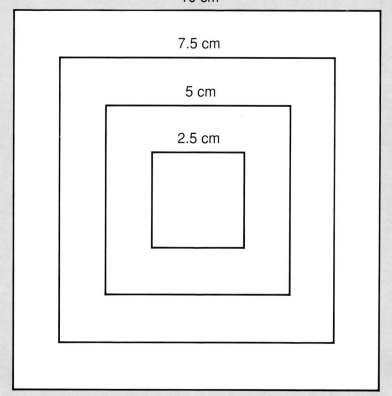

Published by Murdoch Books, a division of Murdoch Magazines Pty Ltd
213 Miller Street, North Sydney, NSW 2060

Project Coordinator: Lisa Johnson
Designer: Steven Dunbar
Project Managing Editor: Susan Tomnay
Commissioned Photography: Jonathan Chester, Greg Slater
Diagrams: Christie and Eckermann, Steven Dunbar

Publisher: Anne Wilson
Publishing Manager: Mark Newman
Production Coordinator: Catie Ziller
Murdoch Books Managing Editor: Susan Tomnay
Marketing Manager: Mark Smith
National Sales Manager: Keith Watson

National Library of Australia
Cataloguing-in-Publication Data
[Better homes and gardens] Joy of patchwork
Includes index
ISBN 0 86411 193 2.
I. Patchwork – Patterns. I. Title: The joy of patchwork.
(Series: Better homes and gardens homemaker library).
746.46041

First published in 1992
Reprinted 1994.
Printed by Prestige Litho, Queensland.
© Murdoch Books

Australian distribution to supermarkets and newsagents by
Gordon & Gotch Ltd, 68 Kingsgrove Road, Belmore NSW 2192

Cover: Checking with Ivy, see page 18
Endpapers: New Antique, Fay Parkes. 230 x 280 cm, 1990
Opposite title page: Table Top Still Life II, Deborah Brearley. 82 x 114 cm, 1991